DEAD MEMORY™

Written and drawn by

MARC-ANTOINE MATHIEU

Lighting assistant
Christel Colas

Hand lettering
Dirk Rehm

English translation
Helge Dascher

DARK HORSE BOOKS

editor
Diana Schutz

design
David Nestelle

digital production
Jason Hvam

publisher
Mike Richardson

Published by
Dark Horse Books
A division of Dark Horse Comics, Inc.
10956 SE Main Street
Milwaukie, Oregon 97222

First Dark Horse edition: October 2003
ISBN 1-56971-840-7

1 3 5 7 9 10 8 6 4 2
Printed in China

PROLOGUE

RECTILINEAR RUINS

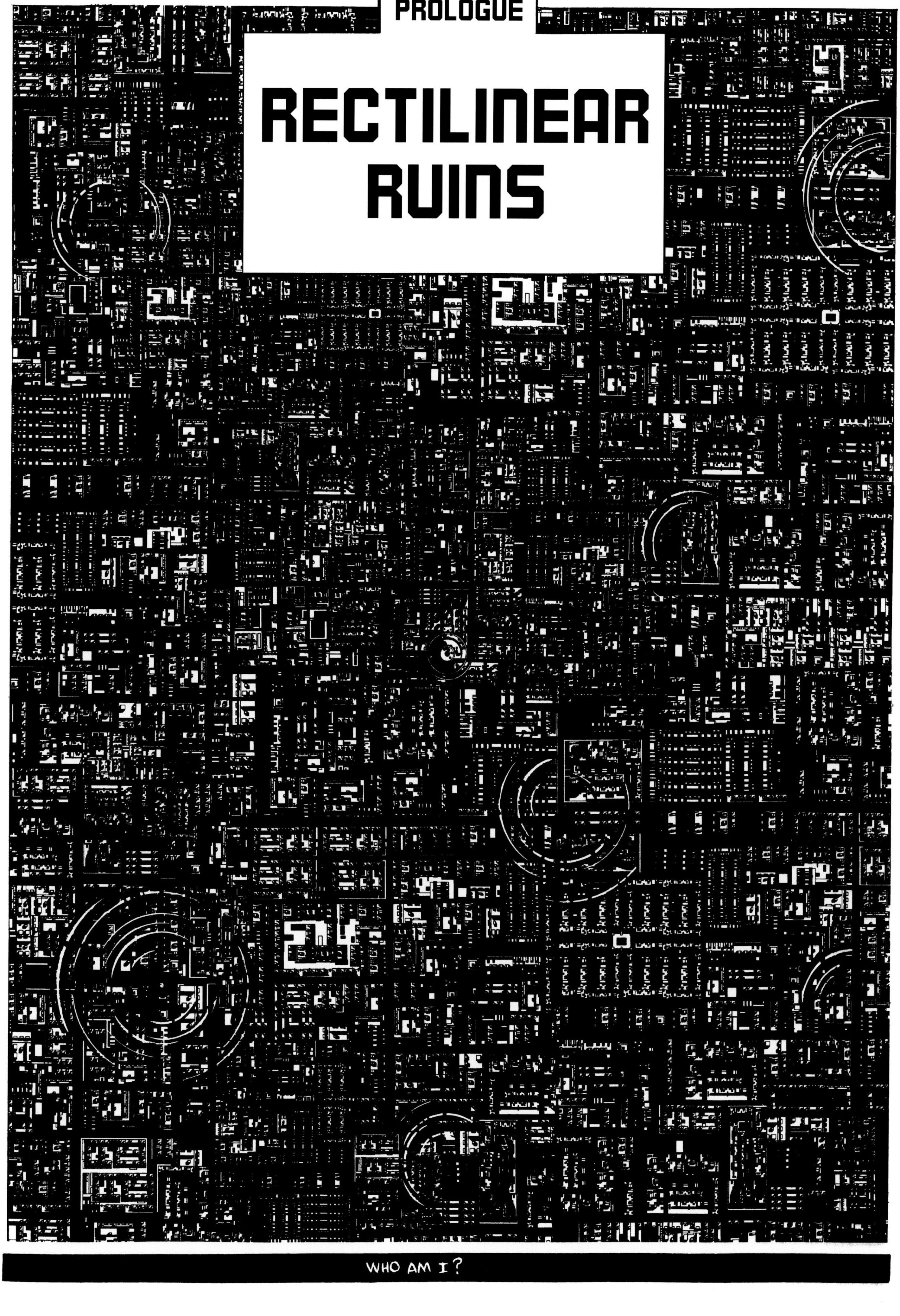
WHO AM I?

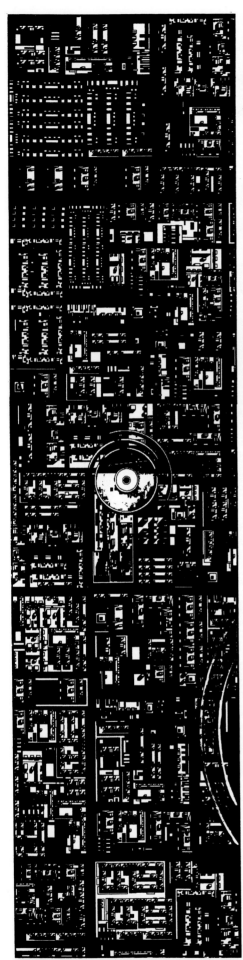

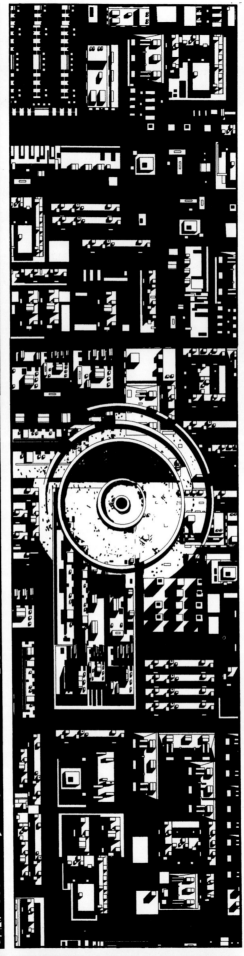

WHO AM I?
YOU WANT TO KNOW
WHO I AM?

ALL RIGHT... I'LL TELL YOU.
BUT FIRST, LET ME TELL YOU WHO
YOU ARE...

... AND WHAT YOU HAVE BECOME.
ALLOW ME TO REVIEW THE
FACTS...

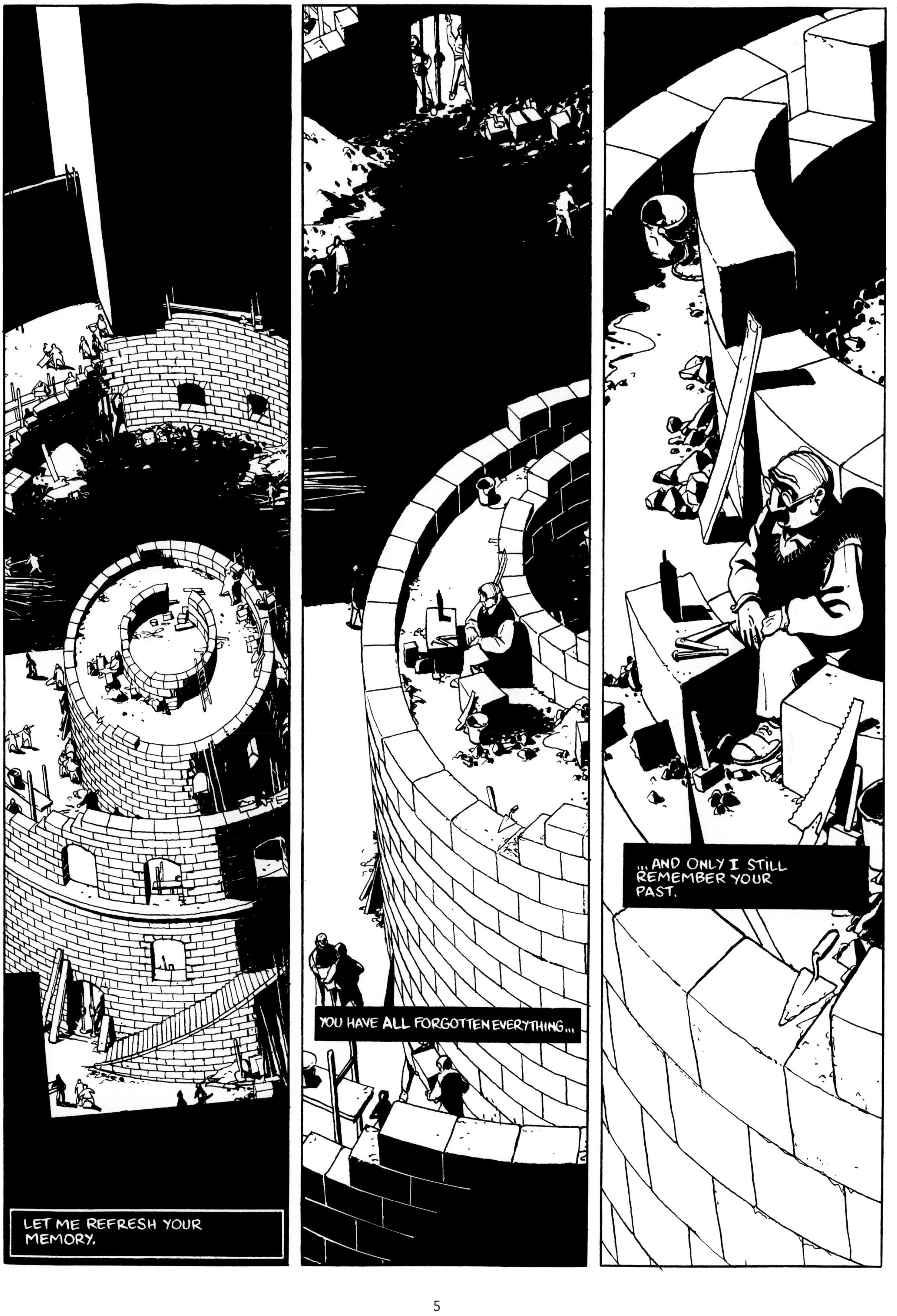
LET ME REFRESH YOUR MEMORY.
YOU HAVE ALL FORGOTTEN EVERYTHING...
... AND ONLY I STILL REMEMBER YOUR PAST.

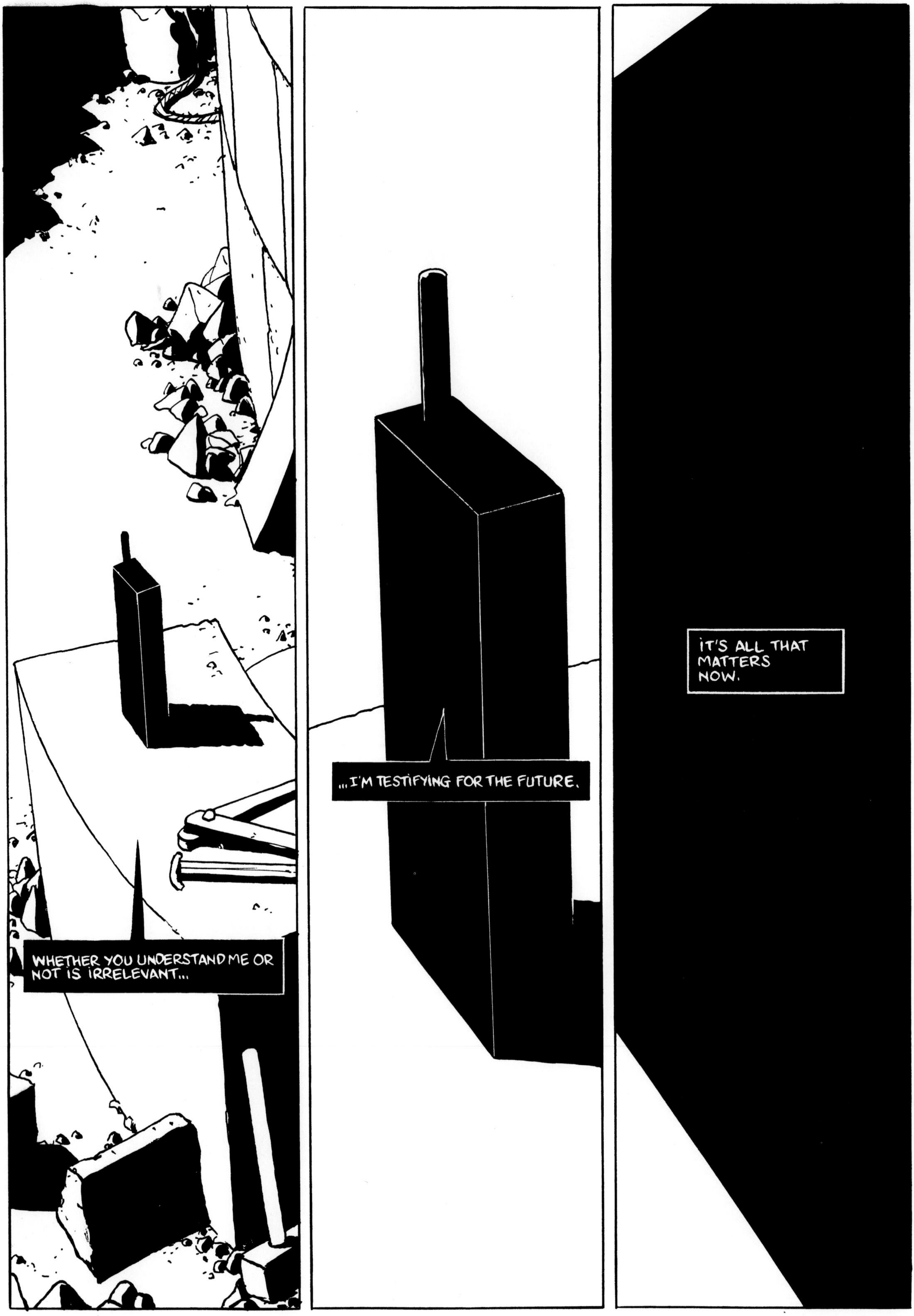
WHETHER YOU UNDERSTAND ME OR NOT IS IRRELEVANT...
...I'M TESTIFYING FOR THE FUTURE.
IT'S ALL THAT MATTERS NOW.

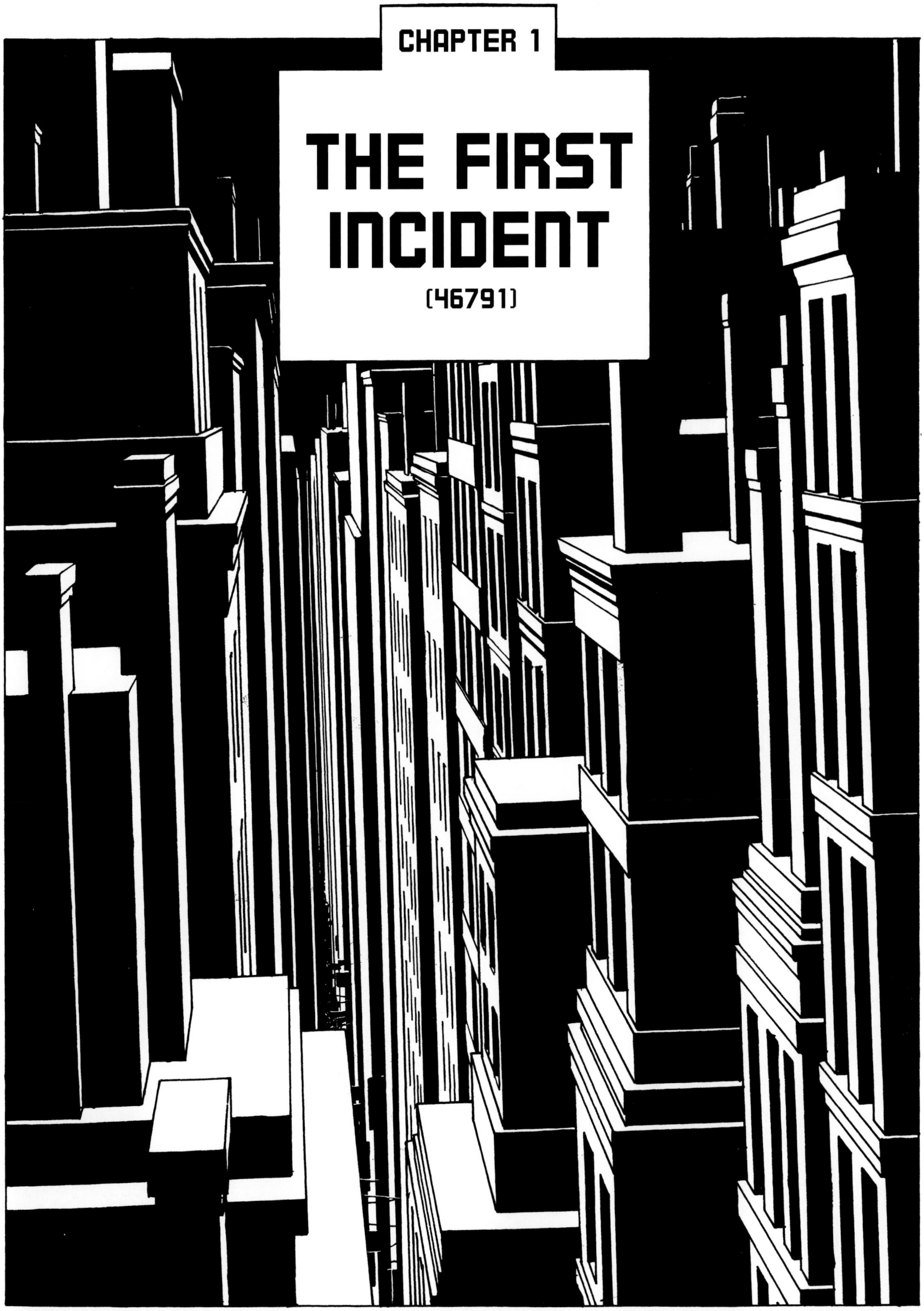
CHAPTER 1
THE FIRST INCIDENT
(46791)
REMEMBER THE CITY... THE WAY IT USED TO BE...

THE CITY... OR HAVE YOU FORGOTTEN THAT WORD, TOO?

THE CITY-- SO STABLE, SO STRUCTURED ...YET... SO COMPLEX.

TOO COMPLEX... LIKE A BUILDING THAT IS TOO TALL AND TOO OLD, WHOSE FOUNDATIONS HAVE BEEN NEGLECTED OVER TIME.

WORST OF ALL IS THE TOTAL LACK OF BOUNDARIES...

I DIDN'T SEE IT MYSELF AT THE TIME.

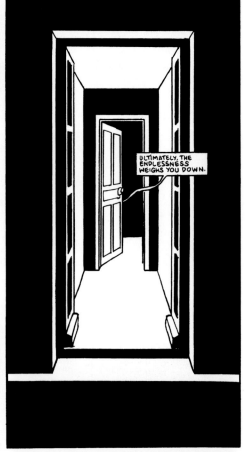

ULTIMATELY, THE ENDLESSNESS WEIGHS YOU DOWN.

I WAS TOO... INVOLVED.

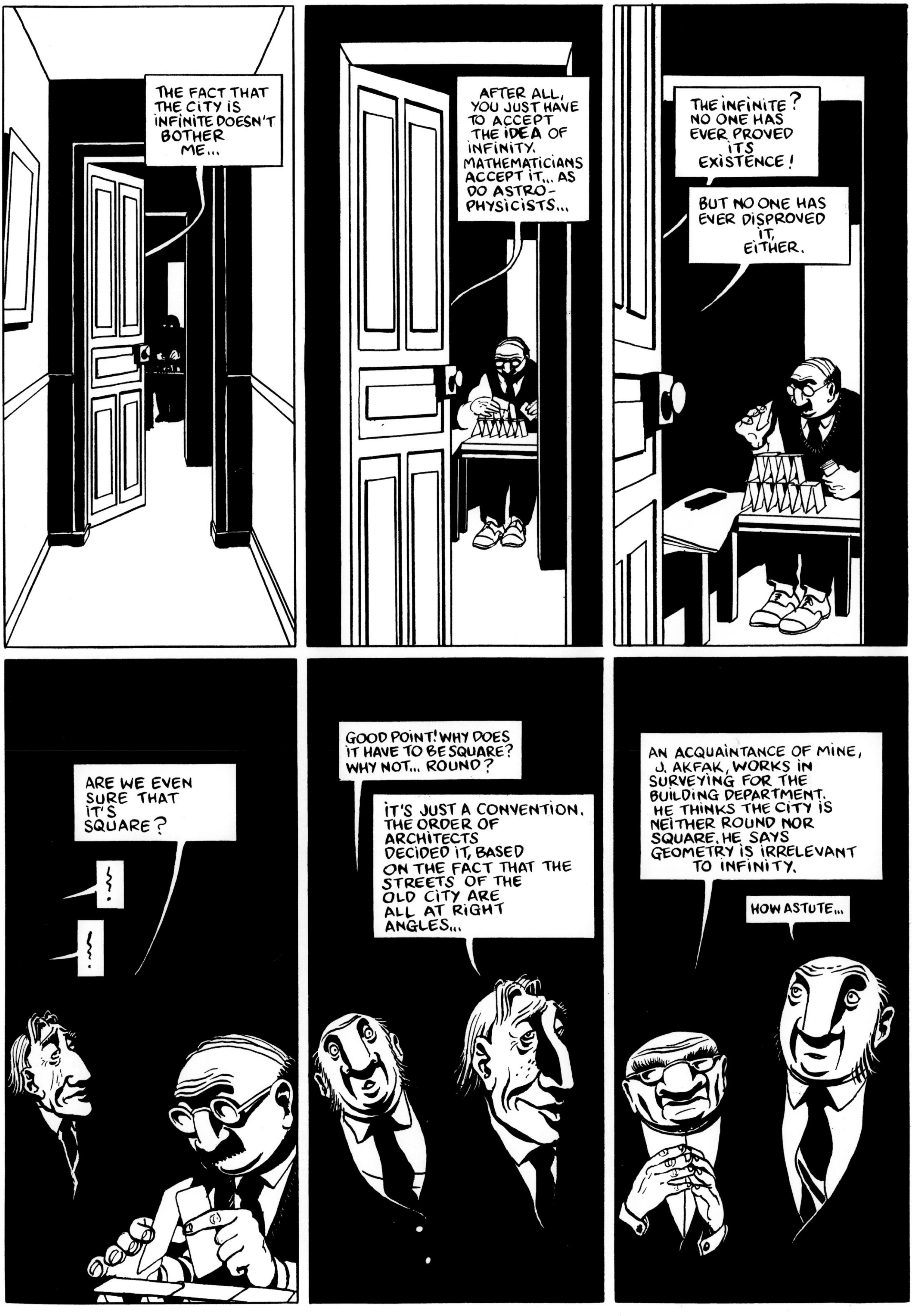
THE FACT THAT THE CITY IS INFINITE DOESN'T BOTHER ME...
AFTER ALL, YOU JUST HAVE TO ACCEPT THE IDEA OF INFINITY. MATHEMATICIANS ACCEPT IT... AS DO ASTRO-PHYSICISTS...
THE INFINITE? NO ONE HAS EVER PROVED ITS EXISTENCE!
BUT NO ONE HAS EVER DISPROVED IT, EITHER.
ARE WE EVEN SURE THAT IT'S SQUARE?
¿
¡
GOOD POINT! WHY DOES IT HAVE TO BE SQUARE? WHY NOT... ROUND?
IT'S JUST A CONVENTION. THE ORDER OF ARCHITECTS DECIDED IT, BASED ON THE FACT THAT THE STREETS OF THE OLD CITY ARE ALL AT RIGHT ANGLES...
AN ACQUAINTANCE OF MINE, J. AKFAK, WORKS IN SURVEYING FOR THE BUILDING DEPARTMENT. HE THINKS THE CITY IS NEITHER ROUND NOR SQUARE. HE SAYS GEOMETRY IS IRRELEVANT TO INFINITY.
HOW ASTUTE...

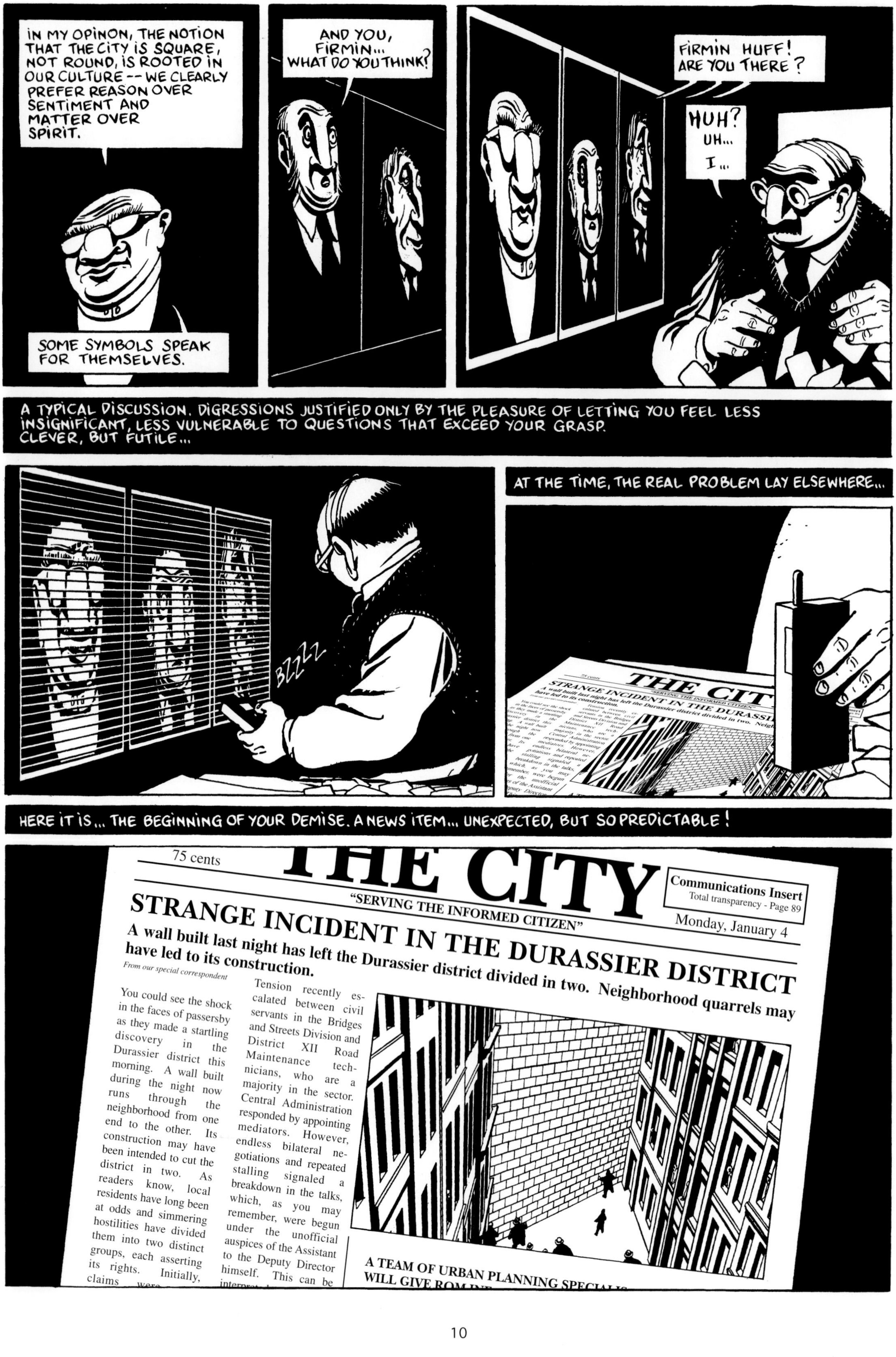
IN MY OPINON, THE NOTION THAT THE CITY IS SQUARE, NOT ROUND, IS ROOTED IN OUR CULTURE -- WE CLEARLY PREFER REASON OVER SENTIMENT AND MATTER OVER SPIRIT.
SOME SYMBOLS SPEAK FOR THEMSELVES.
AND YOU, FIRMIN... WHAT DO YOU THINK?
FIRMIN HUFF! ARE YOU THERE?
HUH? UH... I...
A TYPICAL DISCUSSION. DIGRESSIONS JUSTIFIED ONLY BY THE PLEASURE OF LETTING YOU FEEL LESS INSIGNIFICANT, LESS VULNERABLE TO QUESTIONS THAT EXCEED YOUR GRASP. CLEVER, BUT FUTILE...
BZZZZ
AT THE TIME, THE REAL PROBLEM LAY ELSEWHERE...
HERE IT IS... THE BEGINNING OF YOUR DEMISE. A NEWS ITEM... UNEXPECTED, BUT SO PREDICTABLE!
75 cents
THE CITY
"SERVING THE INFORMED CITIZEN"
Communications Insert
Total transparency - Page 89
Monday, January 4
STRANGE INCIDENT IN THE DURASSIER DISTRICT
A wall built last night has left the Durassier district divided in two. Neighborhood quarrels may have led to its construction.
From our special correspondent
You could see the shock in the faces of passersby as they made a startling discovery in the Durassier district this morning. A wall built during the night now runs through the neighborhood from one end to the other. Its construction may have been intended to cut the district in two. As readers know, local residents have long been at odds and simmering hostilities have divided them into two distinct groups, each asserting its rights. Initially,
Tension recently escalated between civil servants in the Bridges and Streets Division and District XII Road Maintenance technicians, who are a majority in the sector. Central Administration responded by appointing mediators. However, endless bilateral negotiations and repeated stalling signaled a breakdown in the talks, which, as you may remember, were begun under the unofficial auspices of the Assistant to the Deputy Director himself. This can be
A TEAM OF URBAN PLANNING
WILL GIVE

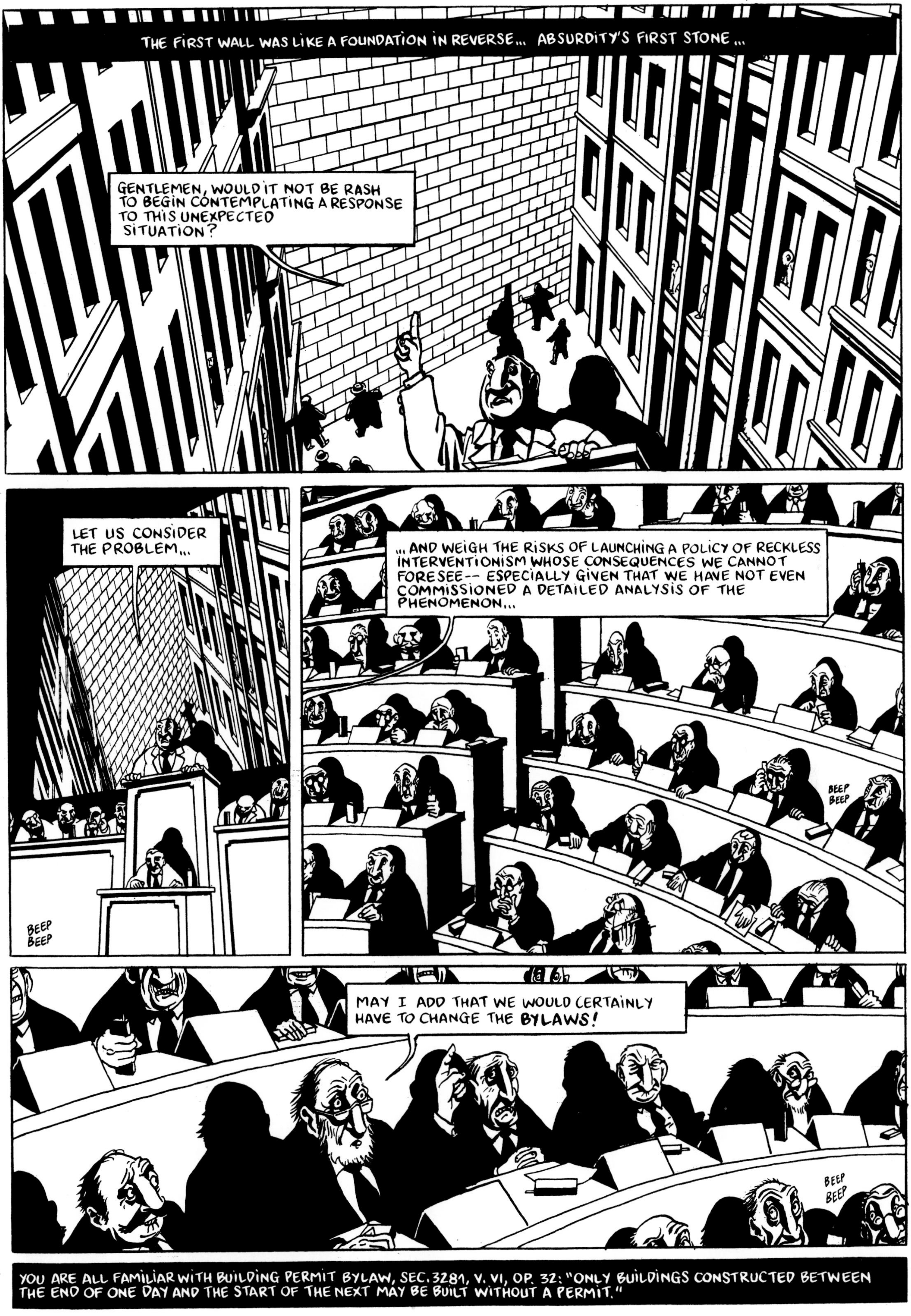
THE FIRST WALL WAS LIKE A FOUNDATION IN REVERSE... ABSURDITY'S FIRST STONE...
GENTLEMEN, WOULD IT NOT BE RASH TO BEGIN CONTEMPLATING A RESPONSE TO THIS UNEXPECTED SITUATION?
LET US CONSIDER THE PROBLEM...
BEEP BEEP
...AND WEIGH THE RISKS OF LAUNCHING A POLICY OF RECKLESS INTERVENTIONISM WHOSE CONSEQUENCES WE CANNOT FORESEE-- ESPECIALLY GIVEN THAT WE HAVE NOT EVEN COMMISSIONED A DETAILED ANALYSIS OF THE PHENOMENON...
BEEP BEEP
MAY I ADD THAT WE WOULD CERTAINLY HAVE TO CHANGE THE BYLAWS!
BEEP BEEP
YOU ARE ALL FAMILIAR WITH BUILDING PERMIT BYLAW, SEC. 3281, V. VI, OP. 32: "ONLY BUILDINGS CONSTRUCTED BETWEEN THE END OF ONE DAY AND THE START OF THE NEXT MAY BE BUILT WITHOUT A PERMIT."

IF THAT'S THE CASE, GIVEN THE NUMBER OF PROPOSALS, COUNTER-PROPOSALS, AMENDMENTS, AND FOLLOW-UP AMENDMENTS, WE WON'T GET AROUND TO SERIOUS RESOLUTIONS TO CHANGE THE LAW FOR ANOTHER SIX MONTHS...

WHY NOT PASS SPECIAL LEGISLATION?

HMM...
UH...

GENTLEMEN... GIVEN THE COMPLEXITY OF THE SITUATION, IT WOULD BE POLITICALLY UNWISE TO ACT WITH HASTE.

AND... WITHOUT WANTING TO BE OVERLY CAUTIOUS, I THINK WE SHOULD TAKE THINGS ONE STEP AT A TIME. AFTER ALL, IT APPEARS THAT THIS WALL HAS RESTORED PEACE AND ORDER IN THE NEIGHBORHOOD.

ABSO-LUTELY

TRUE

YES

YES

WELL SAID

YES

BEEP

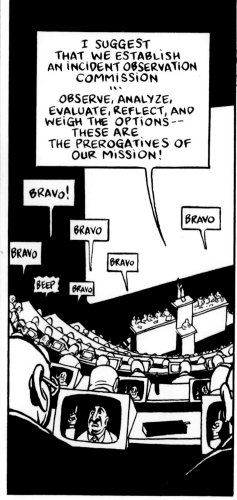

I SUGGEST THAT WE ESTABLISH AN INCIDENT OBSERVATION COMMISSION ... OBSERVE, ANALYZE, EVALUATE, REFLECT, AND WEIGH THE OPTIONS-- THESE ARE THE PREROGATIVES OF OUR MISSION!

BRAVO!

BRAVO

BRAVO

BRAVO

BRAVO

BEEP

BRAVO

CHAPTER 2

THE LAND REGISTRY

(41297)

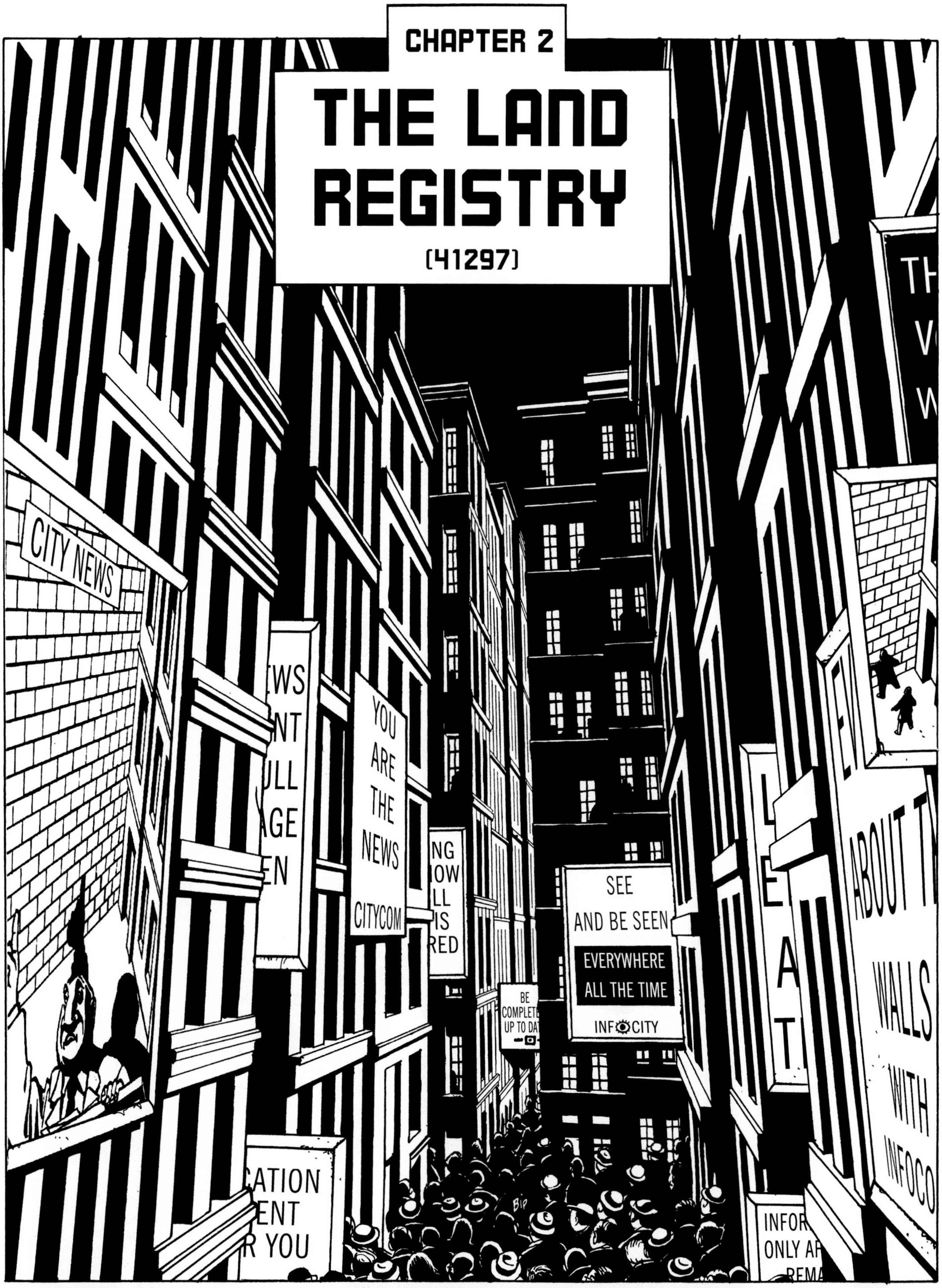
CITY NEWS
YOU ARE THE NEWS
CITYCOM
SEE AND BE SEEN
EVERYWHERE ALL THE TIME
INFOCITY
WALLS WITH

OTHER WALLS APPEARED IN THE MONTHS THAT FOLLOWED... THE FIRST INCIDENT WAS AN IDEAL PRETEXT FOR LATENT HOSTILITIES TO SURFACE. IN THE TRAFFIC DEPARTMENT, PAVING TECHNICIANS SIDED WITH ROAD MAINTENANCE, WHILE TRAFFIC OFFICERS BECAME STAUNCH "BRIDGE AND STREET" SUPPORTERS. TELEPHONE OPERATORS AT THE CENTRAL SWITCHBOARD JOINED THE MAINTENANCE CONTINGENT. IN THE NORTH END, THE RECORDS DEPARTMENT BATTLED WITH THE PLANNING DIVISION...

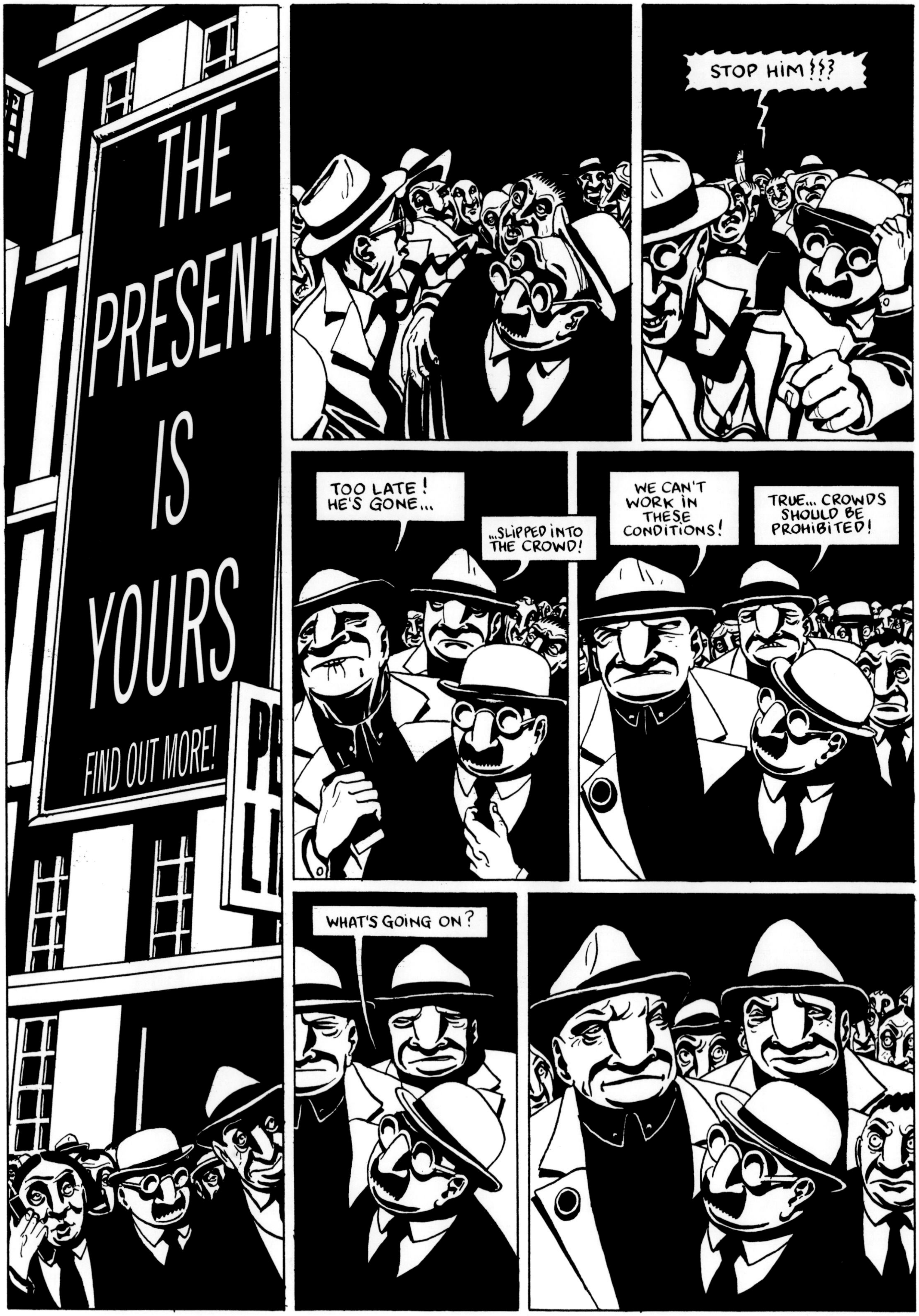
THE PRESENT IS YOURS
FIND OUT MORE!
STOP HIM!??
TOO LATE! HE'S GONE...
...SLIPPED INTO THE CROWD!
WE CAN'T WORK IN THESE CONDITIONS!
TRUE... CROWDS SHOULD BE PROHIBITED!
WHAT'S GOING ON?

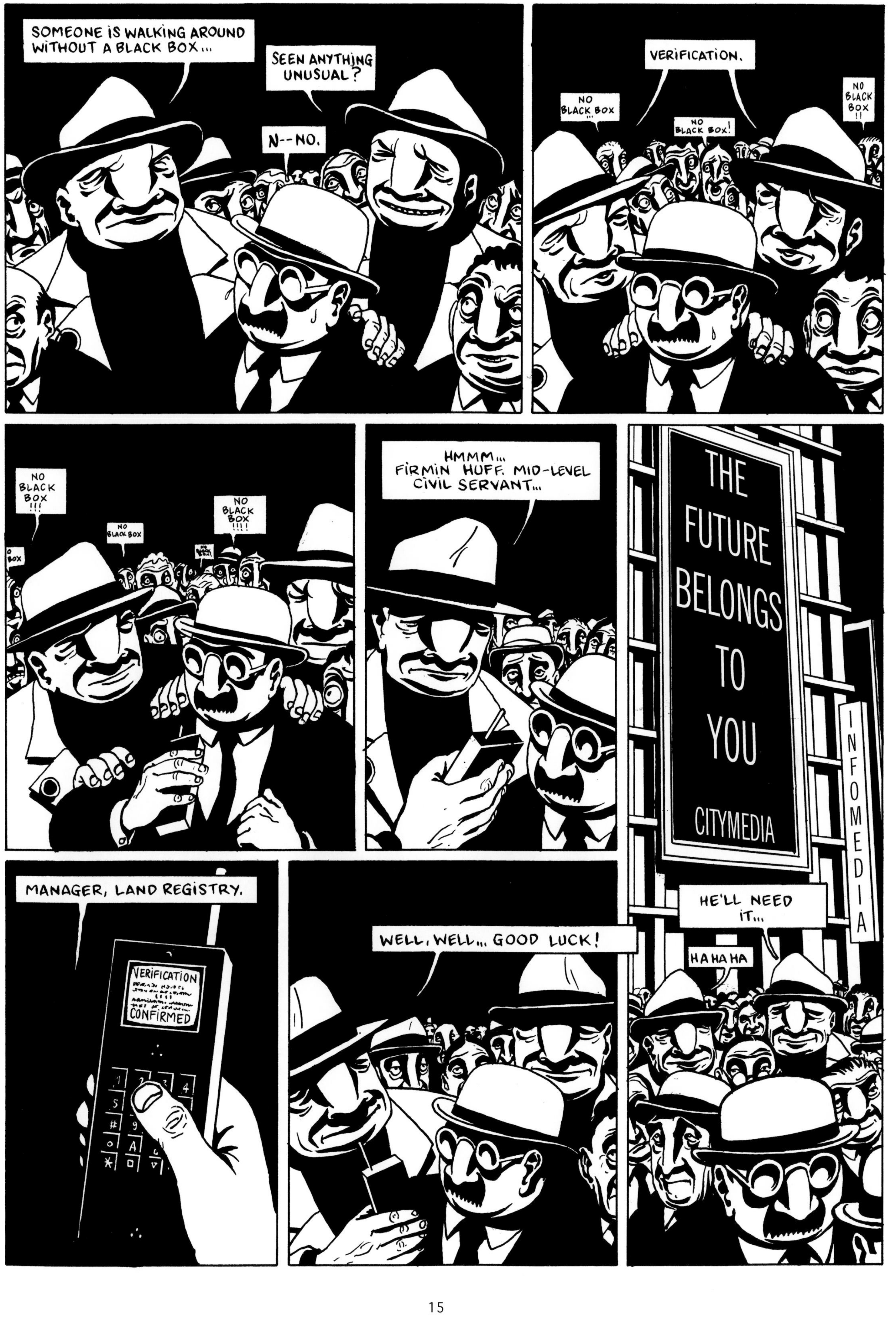
SOMEONE IS WALKING AROUND WITHOUT A BLACK BOX...
SEEN ANYTHING UNUSUAL?
N--NO.
VERIFICATION.
NO BLACK BOX
NO BLACK BOX!
NO BLACK BOX !!
NO BLACK BOX !!!
NO BLACK BOX
NO BLACK BOX !!!!
HMMM... FIRMIN HUFF. MID-LEVEL CIVIL SERVANT...
THE FUTURE BELONGS TO YOU
CITYMEDIA
INFOMEDIA
MANAGER, LAND REGISTRY.
VERIFICATION
CONFIRMED
WELL, WELL... GOOD LUCK!
HE'LL NEED IT...
HA HA HA

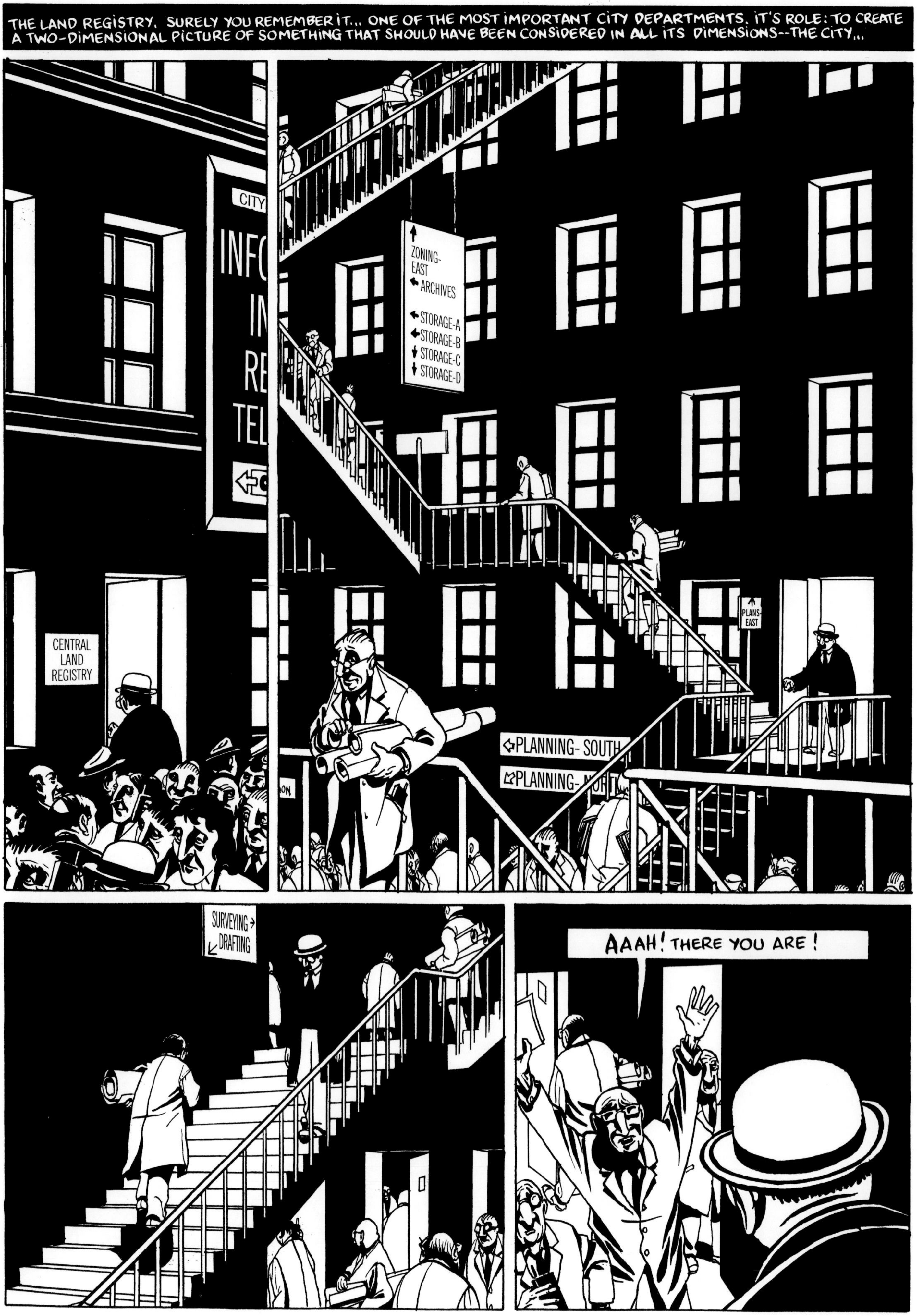
THE LAND REGISTRY. SURELY YOU REMEMBER IT... ONE OF THE MOST IMPORTANT CITY DEPARTMENTS. IT'S ROLE: TO CREATE A TWO-DIMENSIONAL PICTURE OF SOMETHING THAT SHOULD HAVE BEEN CONSIDERED IN ALL ITS DIMENSIONS--THE CITY...
CITY
CENTRAL LAND REGISTRY
ZONING-EAST
ARCHIVES
STORAGE-A
STORAGE-B
STORAGE-C
STORAGE-D
PLANS-EAST
PLANNING- SOUTH
PLANNING-
SURVEYING
DRAFTING
AAAH! THERE YOU ARE!

I DON'T WANT TO SOUND LIKE AN ALARMIST, BUT THE SITUATION IS BECOMING VERY WORRISO--

12 MORE WALLS! LAST NIGHT...

MANAGEMENT CONFLICT ON THE WEST SIDE. THE ASSISTANT DIRECTOR HAS JOINED DISTRICT PROTESTS AGAINST ROAD MAINTENANCE...

THE AUTONOMIST BANKING MOVEMENT HAS CLAIMED RESPONSIBILITY FOR THE WALL AT THE CURRENCY DEPARTMENT.

UNION STRIFE IN SUBDIVISION H22. THE WALL RUNS THROUGH THE BUILDING.

ANOTHER WALL HAS CLOSED OFF THE INDUSTRY BUILDING...

AND ANOTHER IS PARALYZING THE SOUTH WING OF THE ARCHIVES...

...A WALL HAS APPEARED BY CENTRAL SORTING, TOO...

OAK SQUARE: THE WALL RUNS THE LENGTH OF THE STR[E]

ANOTHER WALL IN THE UNITED PARTIES SECTOR...

GARMENT DISTRICT: A WALL RUNS THROUGH THE ALLEY AND IS PREVENTING THE

TRAFFIC IS BLOCKED ON DADA BOULEVARD.

IN THE EAST END!

WE'RE ENTERING LOCATIONS...

...BUT ONLY THOSE WITHIN THE INNER CITY LIMITS...

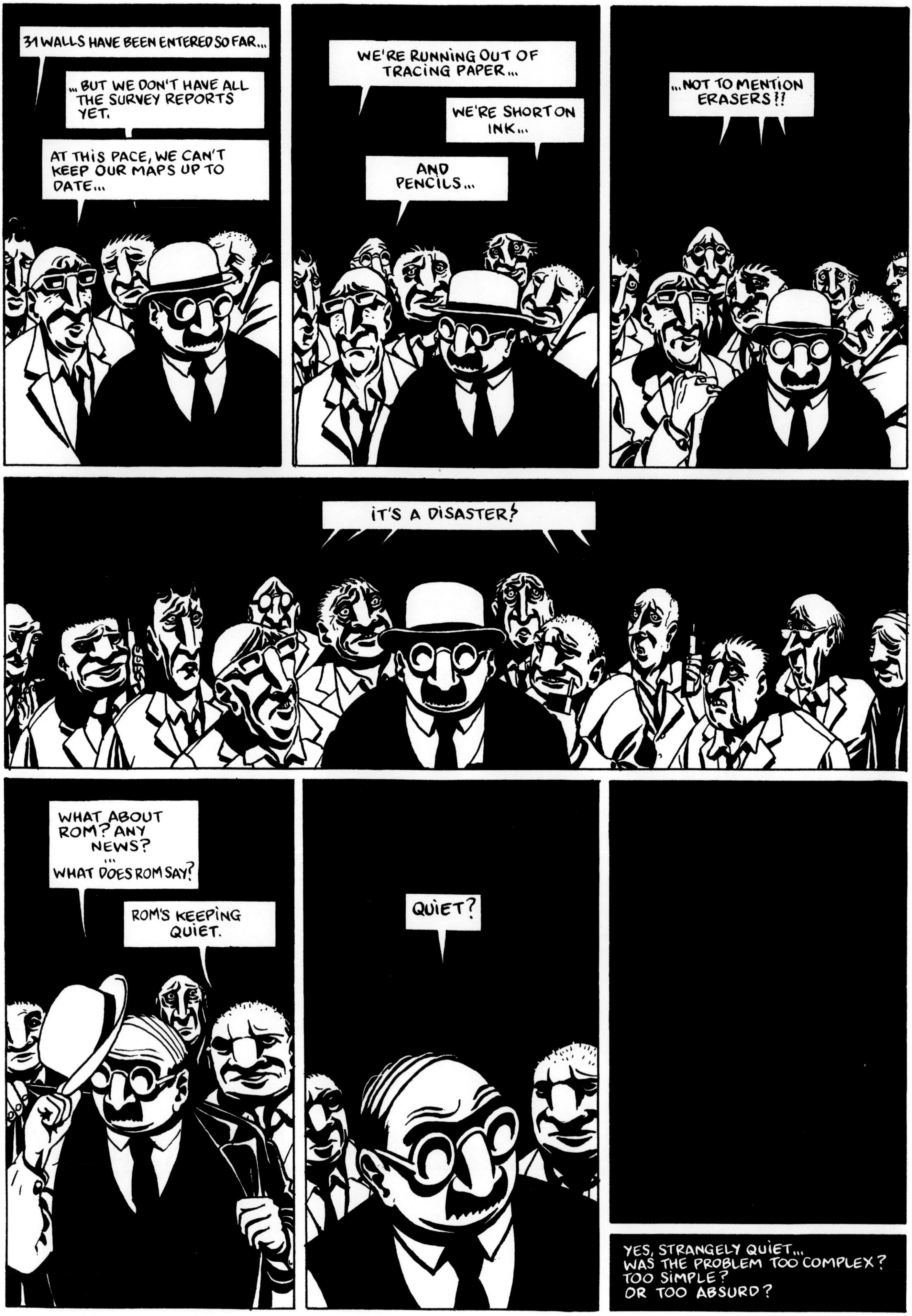

31 WALLS HAVE BEEN ENTERED SO FAR...
... BUT WE DON'T HAVE ALL THE SURVEY REPORTS YET.
AT THIS PACE, WE CAN'T KEEP OUR MAPS UP TO DATE...
WE'RE RUNNING OUT OF TRACING PAPER...
WE'RE SHORT ON INK...
AND PENCILS...
... NOT TO MENTION ERASERS!!
IT'S A DISASTER!
WHAT ABOUT ROM? ANY NEWS? ... WHAT DOES ROM SAY?
ROM'S KEEPING QUIET.
QUIET?
YES, STRANGELY QUIET... WAS THE PROBLEM TOO COMPLEX? TOO SIMPLE? OR TOO ABSURD?

CHAPTER 3

THE OBSERVERS

(23371)

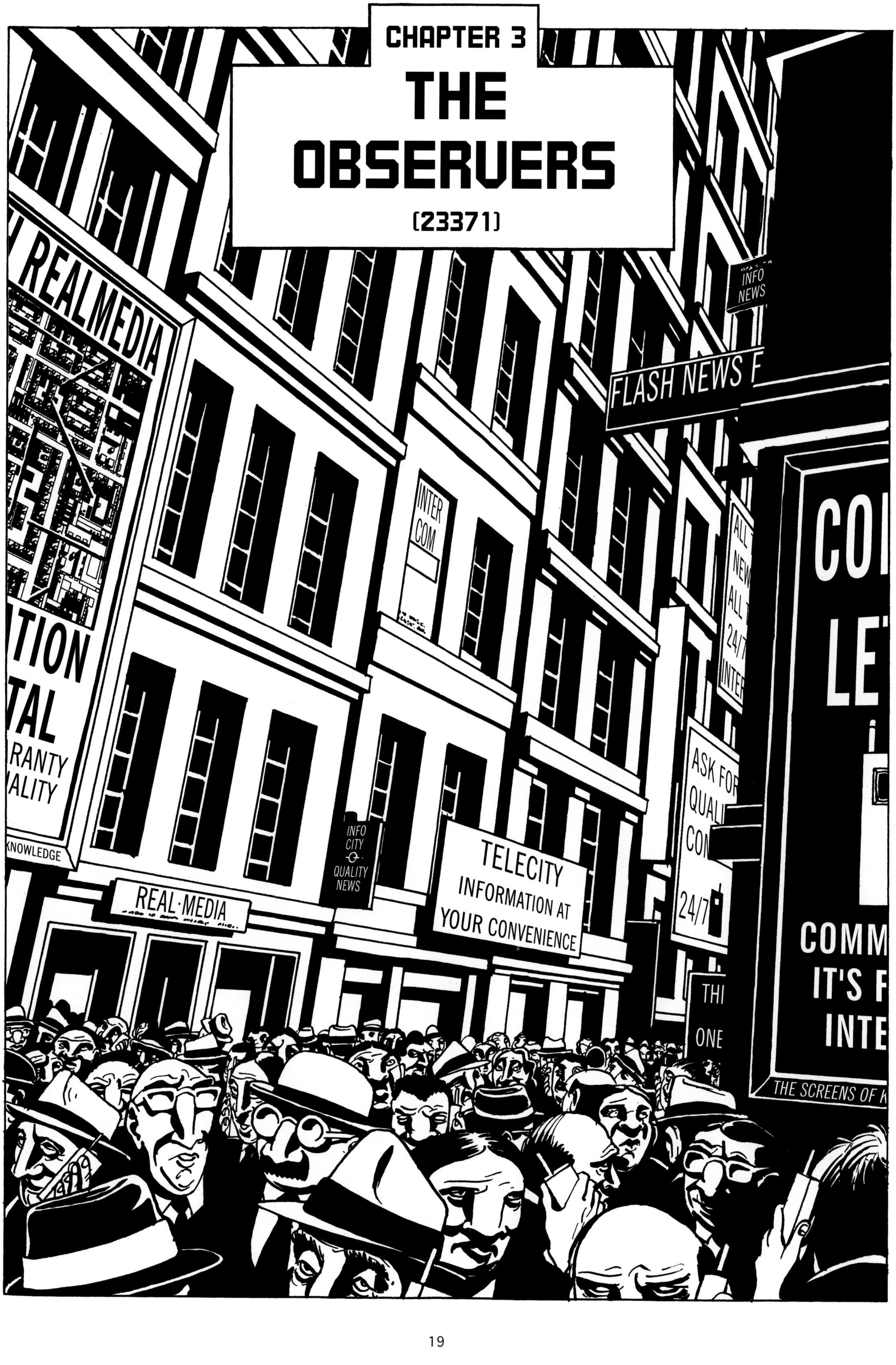
INFO NEWS
FLASH NEWS F
REALMEDIA
TION
TAL
RANTY
ALITY
KNOWLEDGE
INTER COM
REAL·MEDIA
INFO CITY QUALITY NEWS
TELECITY
INFORMATION AT
YOUR CONVENIENCE
ALL NEW ALL T 24/7 INTER
ASK FOR QUALI CO
24/7
THI ONE
CO LE
COMM
IT'S F
INTE
THE SCREENS OF K

WHAT'S GOING ON?
HMM... STRANGE... THIS DOESN'T SEEM LIKE THE USUAL BOTTLENECK...
WE'RE HELD UP...
... I'M SURE HE'LL BE LATE...
THEY'VE CLOSED OFF THE NEIGHBORHOOD...
NO... DON'T WAIT FOR ME...
INFOR
GUARAN
OH, NO! I'M AFRAID THAT...
BRRRRRKRKRRRBRKKRRKRRR
JUST WHAT I THOUGHT!
RKBKRRKB
A GRINDER!!
SEE! IT'S SCHEDULED FOR TODAY AT 4:05 p.m., UPPER HEIGHTS DISTRICT!
RRRKKBRRRKRRRK

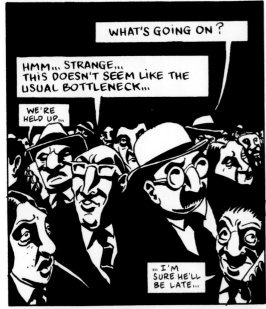

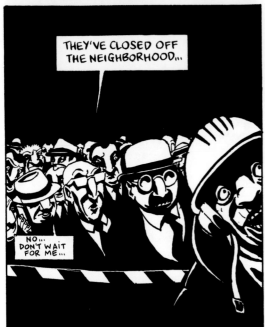

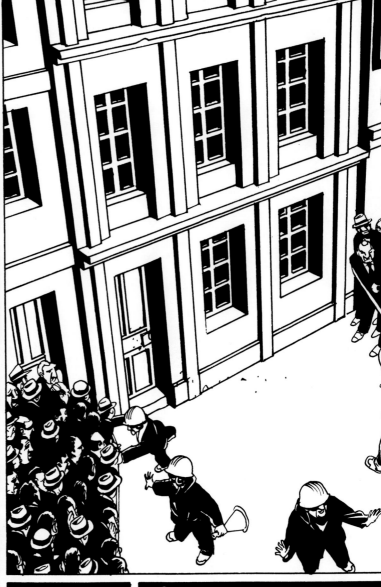

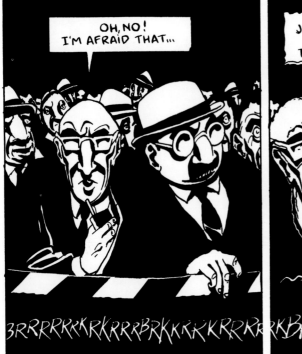

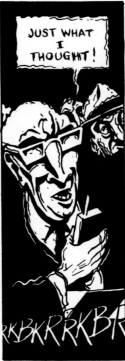

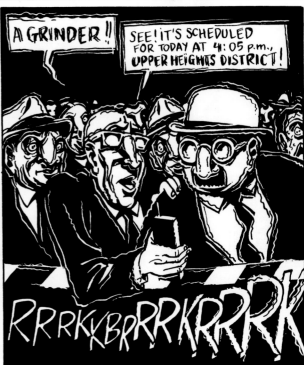

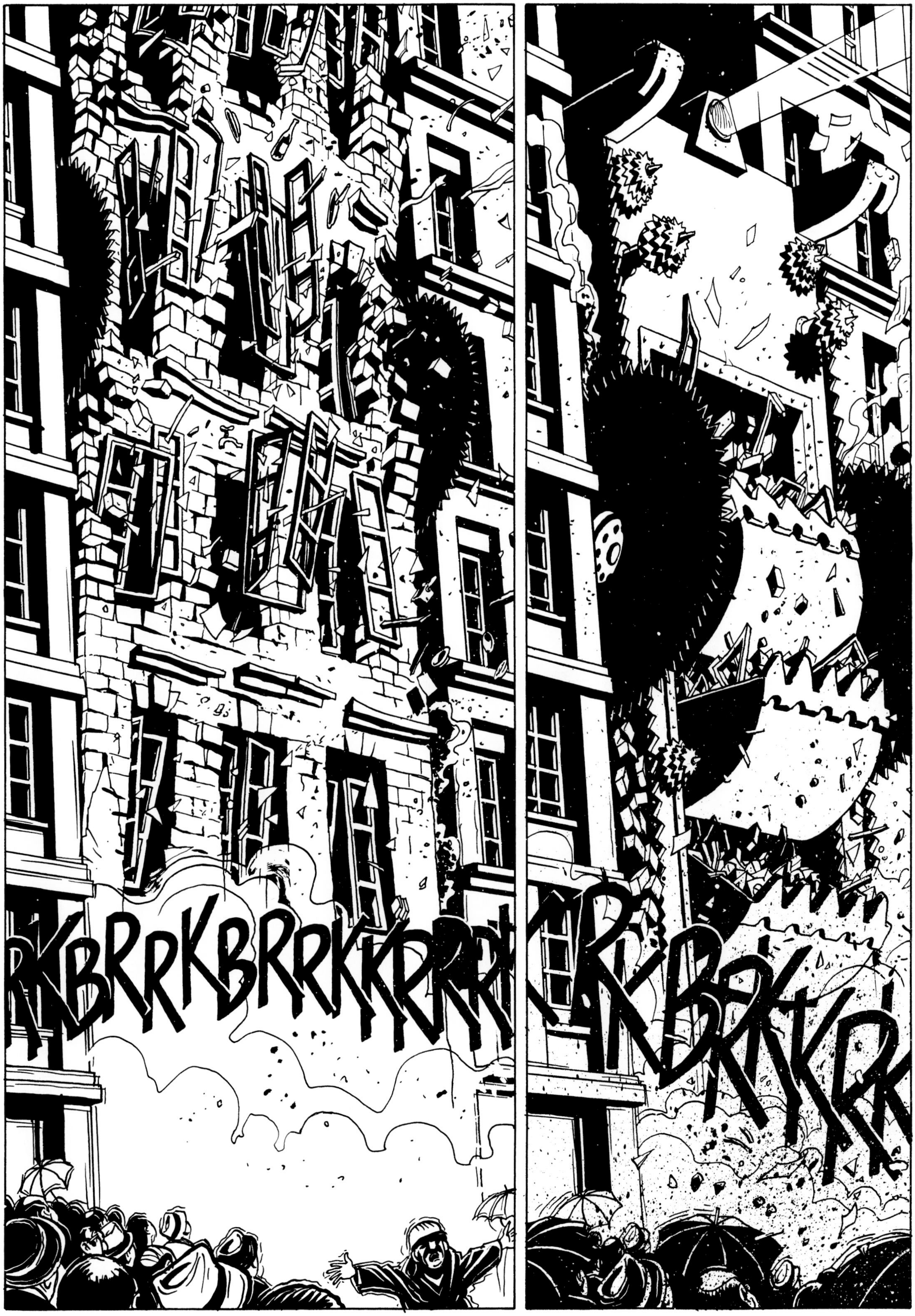
RKBRRKBRRKKRRR
KRRKBRKKRR

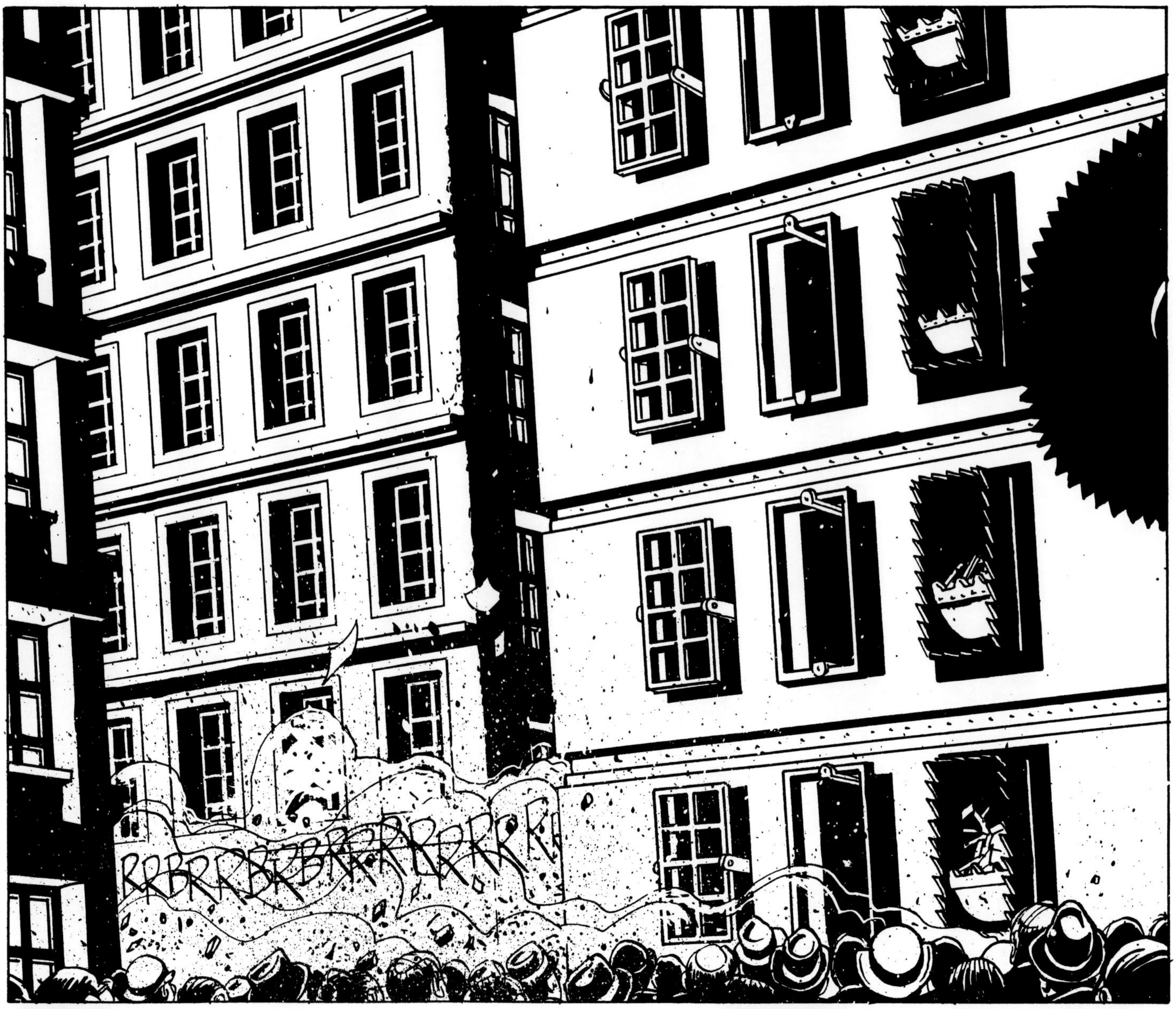

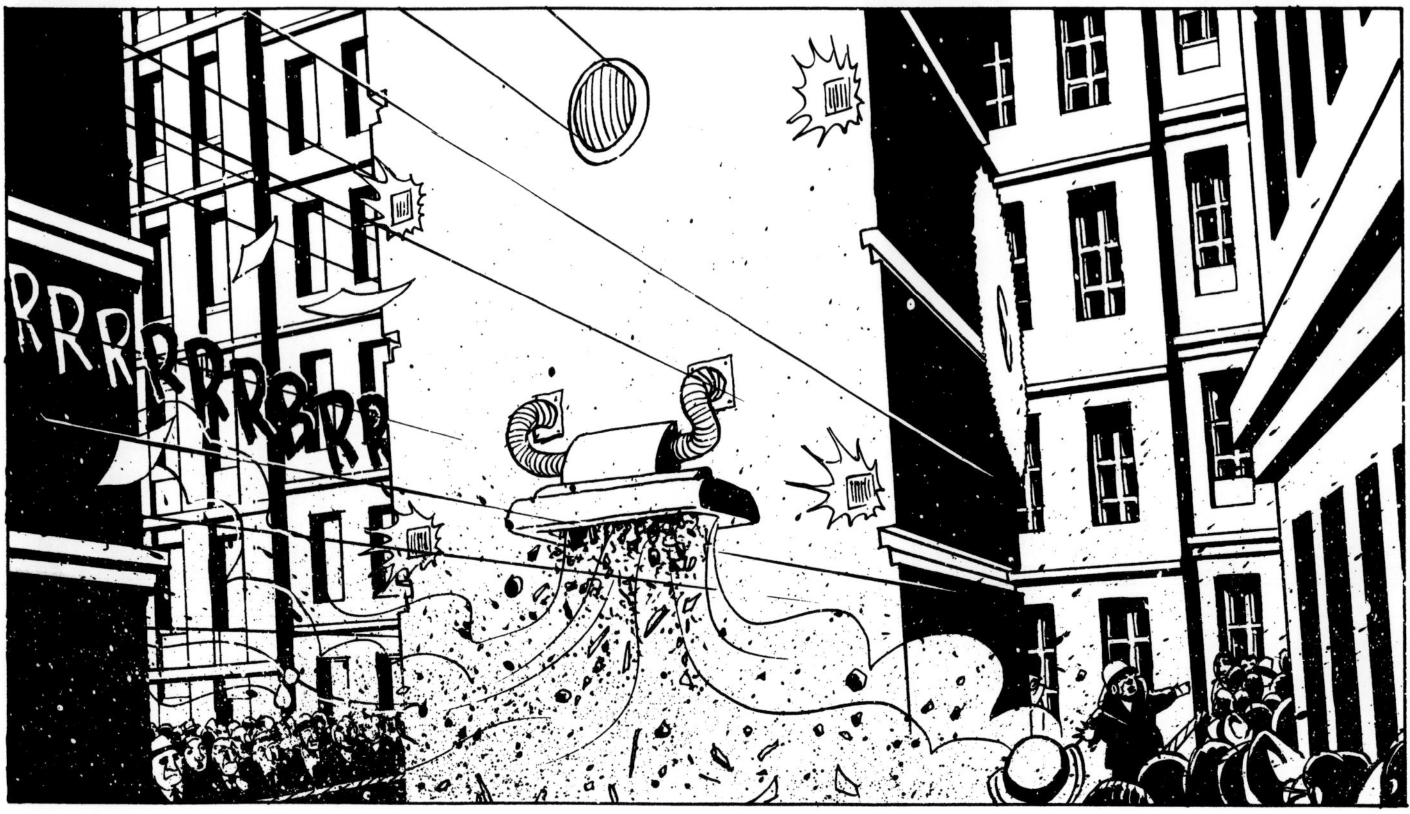

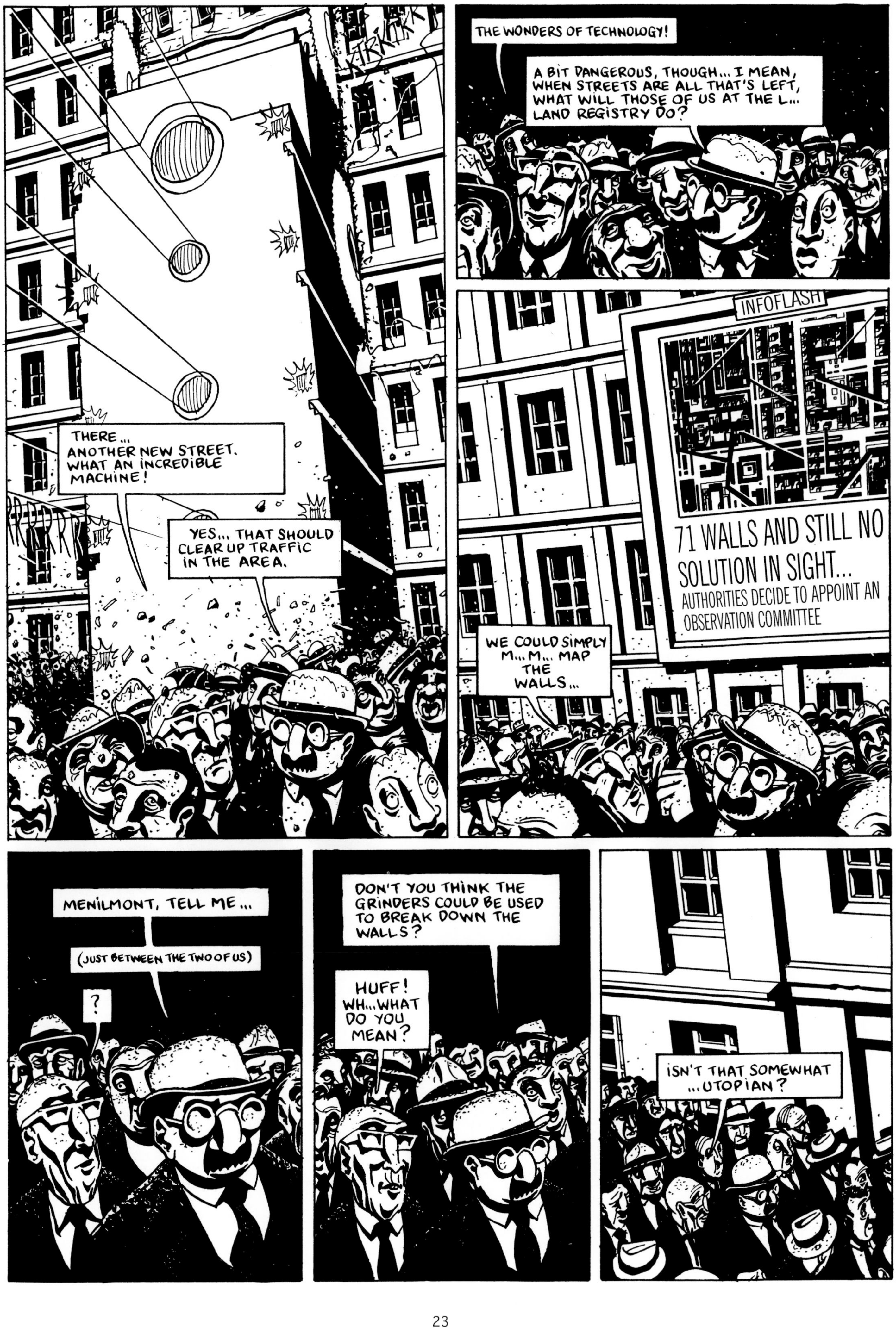

TRRKRR
THERE... ANOTHER NEW STREET. WHAT AN INCREDIBLE MACHINE!
YES... THAT SHOULD CLEAR UP TRAFFIC IN THE AREA.
RRRRRR
THE WONDERS OF TECHNOLOGY!
A BIT DANGEROUS, THOUGH... I MEAN, WHEN STREETS ARE ALL THAT'S LEFT, WHAT WILL THOSE OF US AT THE L... LAND REGISTRY DO?
INFOFLASH
71 WALLS AND STILL NO SOLUTION IN SIGHT...
AUTHORITIES DECIDE TO APPOINT AN OBSERVATION COMMITTEE
WE COULD SIMPLY M... M... MAP THE WALLS...
MENILMONT, TELL ME...
(JUST BETWEEN THE TWO OF US)
?
DON'T YOU THINK THE GRINDERS COULD BE USED TO BREAK DOWN THE WALLS?
HUFF! WH... WHAT DO YOU MEAN?
ISN'T THAT SOMEWHAT ...UTOPIAN?

OH! ARE YOU GOING TO THE OBSERVATORY, TOO?

I...

BiiiP BiiiP BiiiP

BiP. BiP BiiiP

EXCUSE ME...

EXCUSE ME...

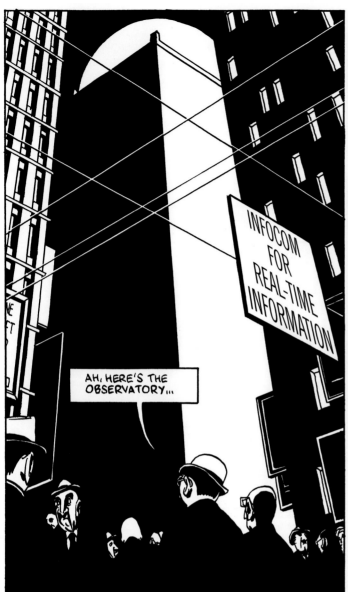

INFOCOM FOR REAL-TIME INFORMATION

AH, HERE'S THE OBSERVATORY...

REMINDER: YOU HAVE A MEETING IN 3 MINUTES AT THE OBSERVATORY WITH MR. HUFF AND MR. BARASSIER.

REMINDER: YOU HAVE A MEETING IN 3 MINUTES AT THE OBSERVATORY WITH MR. MENILMONT AND MR. BARASSIER.

THE WONDERS OF TECHNOLOGY.

MR. HUFF AND MR. MENILMONT, I PRESUME?

M.I.O.P
MINISTERIAL INCIDENT
OBSERVATION POST

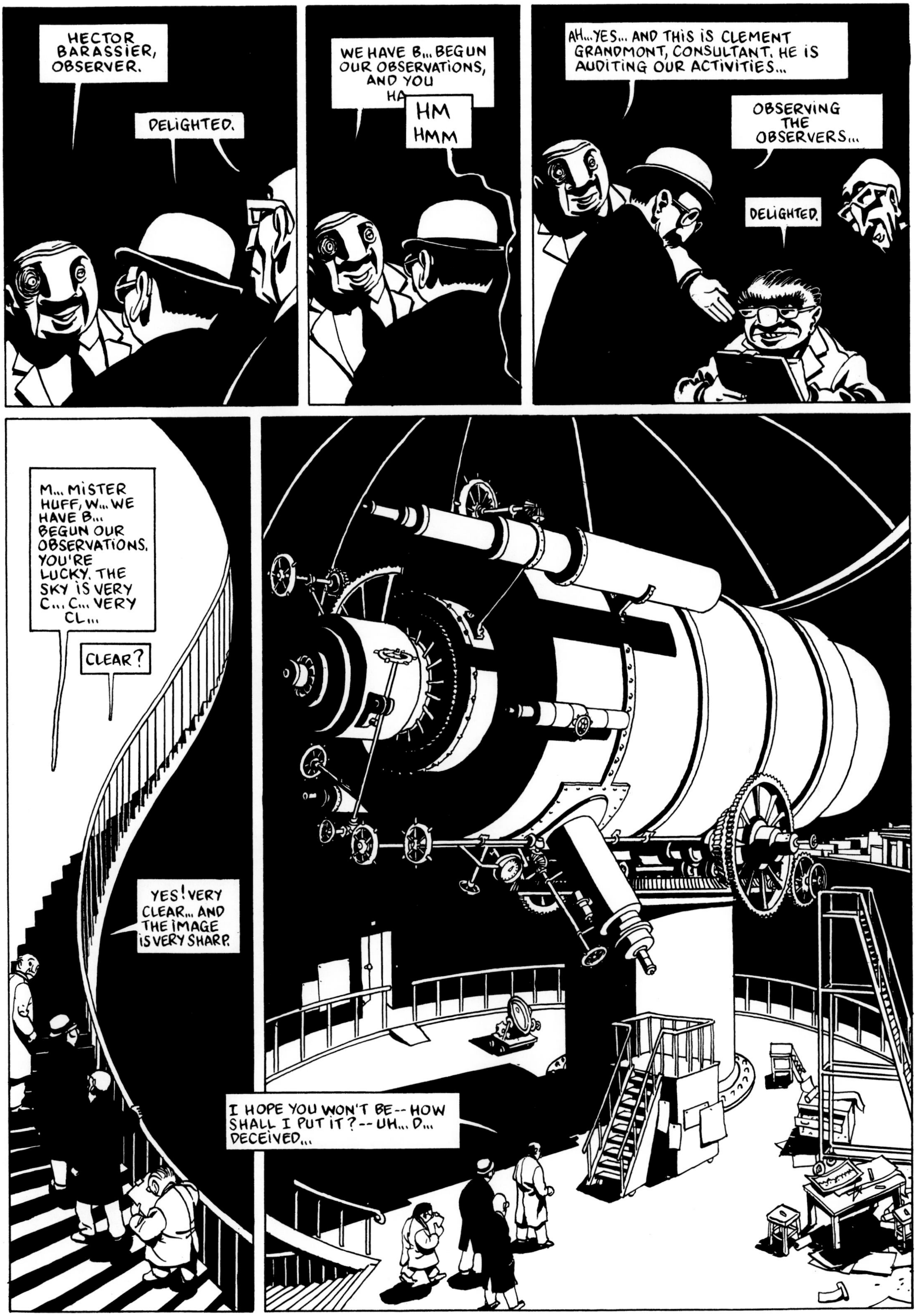
HECTOR BARASSIER, OBSERVER.
DELIGHTED.
WE HAVE B... BEGUN OUR OBSERVATIONS, AND YOU HA
HM HMM
AH... YES... AND THIS IS CLEMENT GRANDMONT, CONSULTANT. HE IS AUDITING OUR ACTIVITIES...
OBSERVING THE OBSERVERS...
DELIGHTED.
M... MISTER HUFF, W... WE HAVE B... BEGUN OUR OBSERVATIONS. YOU'RE LUCKY. THE SKY IS VERY C... C... VERY CL...
CLEAR?
YES! VERY CLEAR... AND THE IMAGE IS VERY SHARP.
I HOPE YOU WON'T BE-- HOW SHALL I PUT IT?-- UH... D... DECEIVED...

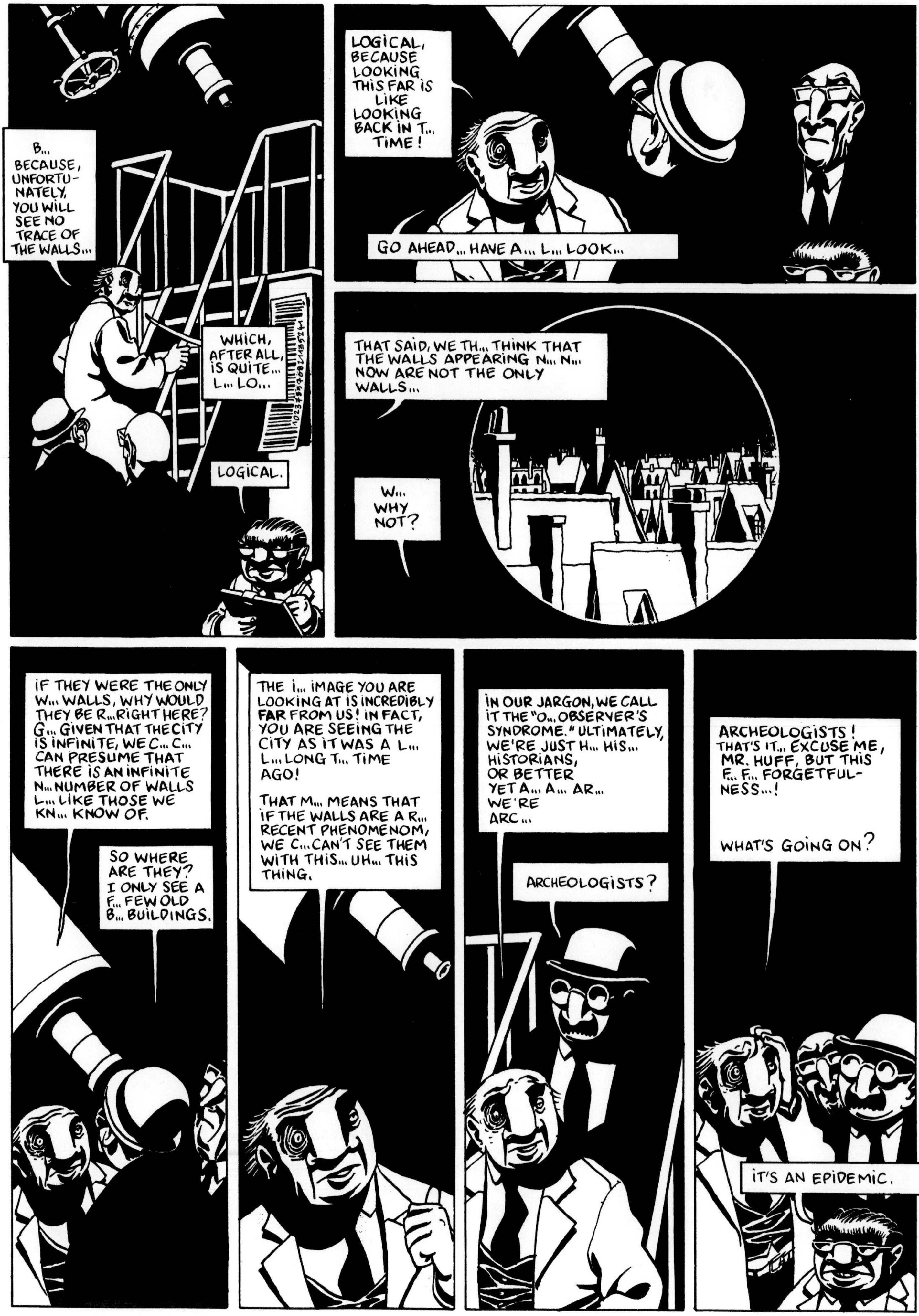
B... BECAUSE, UNFORTUNATELY, YOU WILL SEE NO TRACE OF THE WALLS...
WHICH, AFTER ALL, IS QUITE... L... LO...
LOGICAL.
LOGICAL, BECAUSE LOOKING THIS FAR IS LIKE LOOKING BACK IN T... TIME!
GO AHEAD... HAVE A... L... LOOK...
THAT SAID, WE TH... THINK THAT THE WALLS APPEARING N... N... NOW ARE NOT THE ONLY WALLS...
W... WHY NOT?
IF THEY WERE THE ONLY W... WALLS, WHY WOULD THEY BE R... RIGHT HERE? G... GIVEN THAT THE CITY IS INFINITE, WE C... C... CAN PRESUME THAT THERE IS AN INFINITE N... NUMBER OF WALLS L... LIKE THOSE WE KN... KNOW OF.
SO WHERE ARE THEY? I ONLY SEE A F... FEW OLD B... BUILDINGS.
THE I... IMAGE YOU ARE LOOKING AT IS INCREDIBLY FAR FROM US! IN FACT, YOU ARE SEEING THE CITY AS IT WAS A L... L... LONG T... TIME AGO!
THAT M... MEANS THAT IF THE WALLS ARE A R... RECENT PHENOMENOM, WE C... CAN'T SEE THEM WITH THIS... UH... THIS THING.
IN OUR JARGON, WE CALL IT THE "O... OBSERVER'S SYNDROME." ULTIMATELY, WE'RE JUST H... HIS... HISTORIANS, OR BETTER YET A... A... AR... WE'RE ARC...
ARCHEOLOGISTS?
ARCHEOLOGISTS! THAT'S IT... EXCUSE ME, MR. HUFF, BUT THIS F... F... FORGETFULNESS...!
WHAT'S GOING ON?
IT'S AN EPIDEMIC.

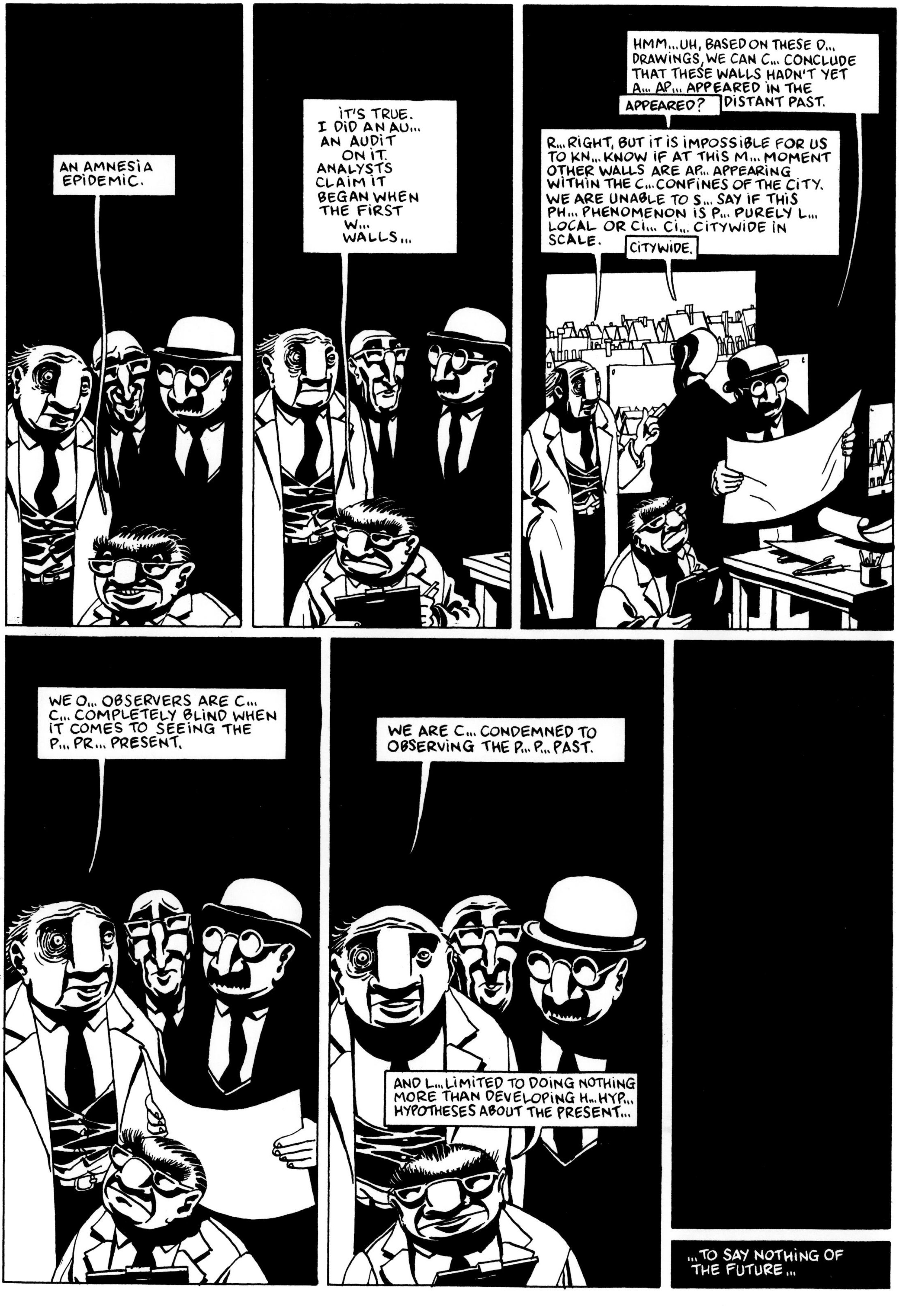
AN AMNESIA EPIDEMIC.
IT'S TRUE. I DID AN AU... AN AUDIT ON IT. ANALYSTS CLAIM IT BEGAN WHEN THE FIRST W... WALLS...
HMM... UH, BASED ON THESE D... DRAWINGS, WE CAN C... CONCLUDE THAT THESE WALLS HADN'T YET A... AP... APPEARED IN THE DISTANT PAST.
APPEARED?
R... RIGHT, BUT IT IS IMPOSSIBLE FOR US TO KN... KNOW IF AT THIS M... MOMENT OTHER WALLS ARE AP... APPEARING WITHIN THE C... CONFINES OF THE CITY. WE ARE UNABLE TO S... SAY IF THIS PH... PHENOMENON IS P... PURELY L... LOCAL OR CI... CI... CITYWIDE IN SCALE.
CITYWIDE.
WE O... OBSERVERS ARE C... C... COMPLETELY BLIND WHEN IT COMES TO SEEING THE P... PR... PRESENT.
WE ARE C... CONDEMNED TO OBSERVING THE P... P... PAST.
AND L... LIMITED TO DOING NOTHING MORE THAN DEVELOPING H... HYP... HYPOTHESES ABOUT THE PRESENT...
...TO SAY NOTHING OF THE FUTURE...

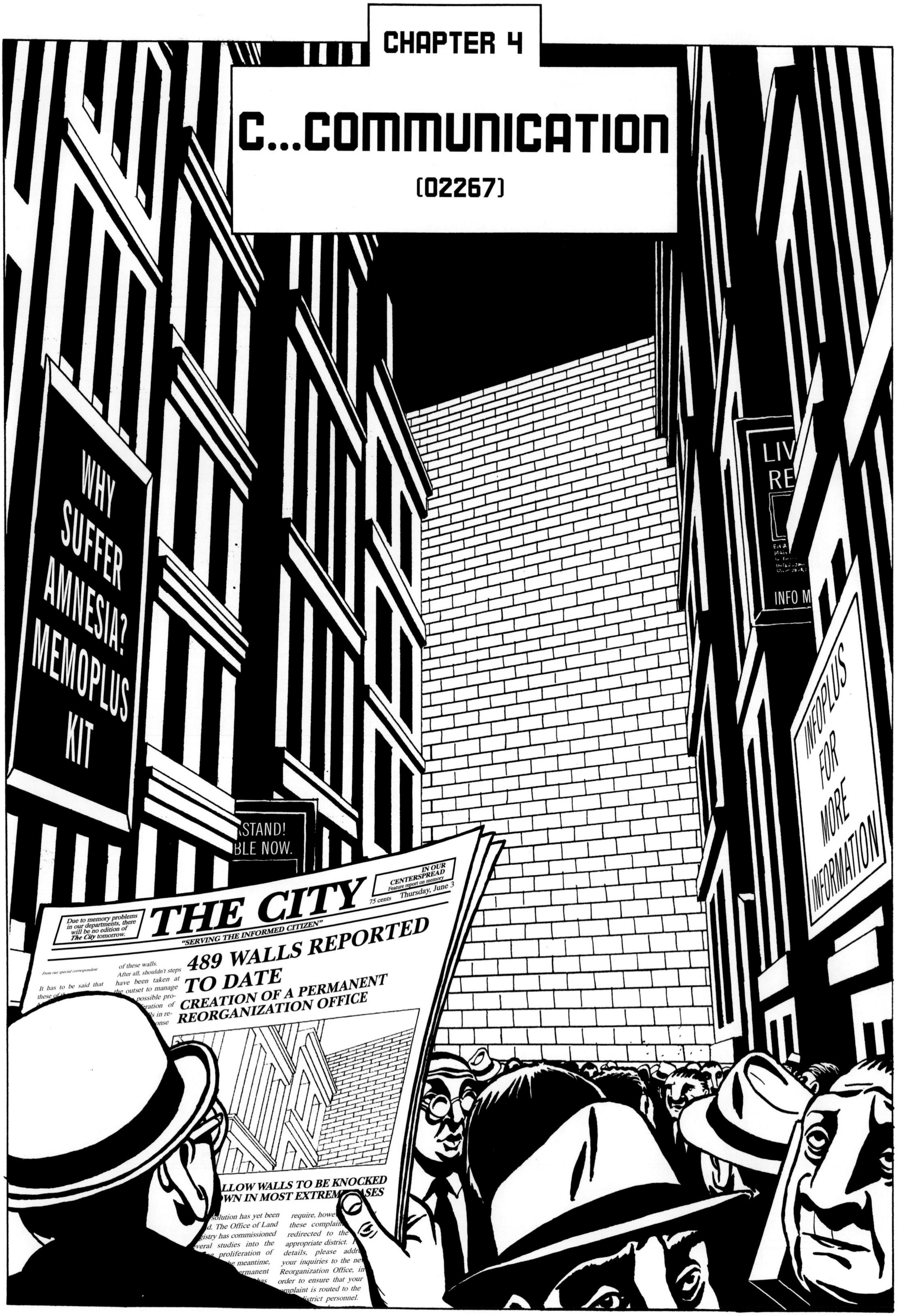
CHAPTER 4
C...COMMUNICATION
(02267)
WHY SUFFER AMNESIA? MEMOPLUS KIT
STAND! BLE NOW.
INFO M
INFOPLUS FOR MORE INFORMATION
THE CITY
"SERVING THE INFORMED CITIZEN"
Due to memory problems in our departments, there will be no edition of The City tomorrow.
IN OUR CENTERSPREAD Feature report on memory
75 cents Thursday, June 3
489 WALLS REPORTED TO DATE
CREATION OF A PERMANENT REORGANIZATION OFFICE
From our special correspondent
It has to be said that
of these walls. After all, shouldn't steps have been taken at the outset to manage
LLOW WALLS TO BE KNOCKED
WN IN MOST EXTREM ASES
solution has yet been
d. The Office of Land
gistry has commissioned
several studies into the
proliferation of
the meantime,
require, howe
these complain
redirected to the
appropriate district.
details, please addr
your inquiries to the ne
Reorganization Office, in
order to ensure that your
mplaint is routed to the
istrict personnel.

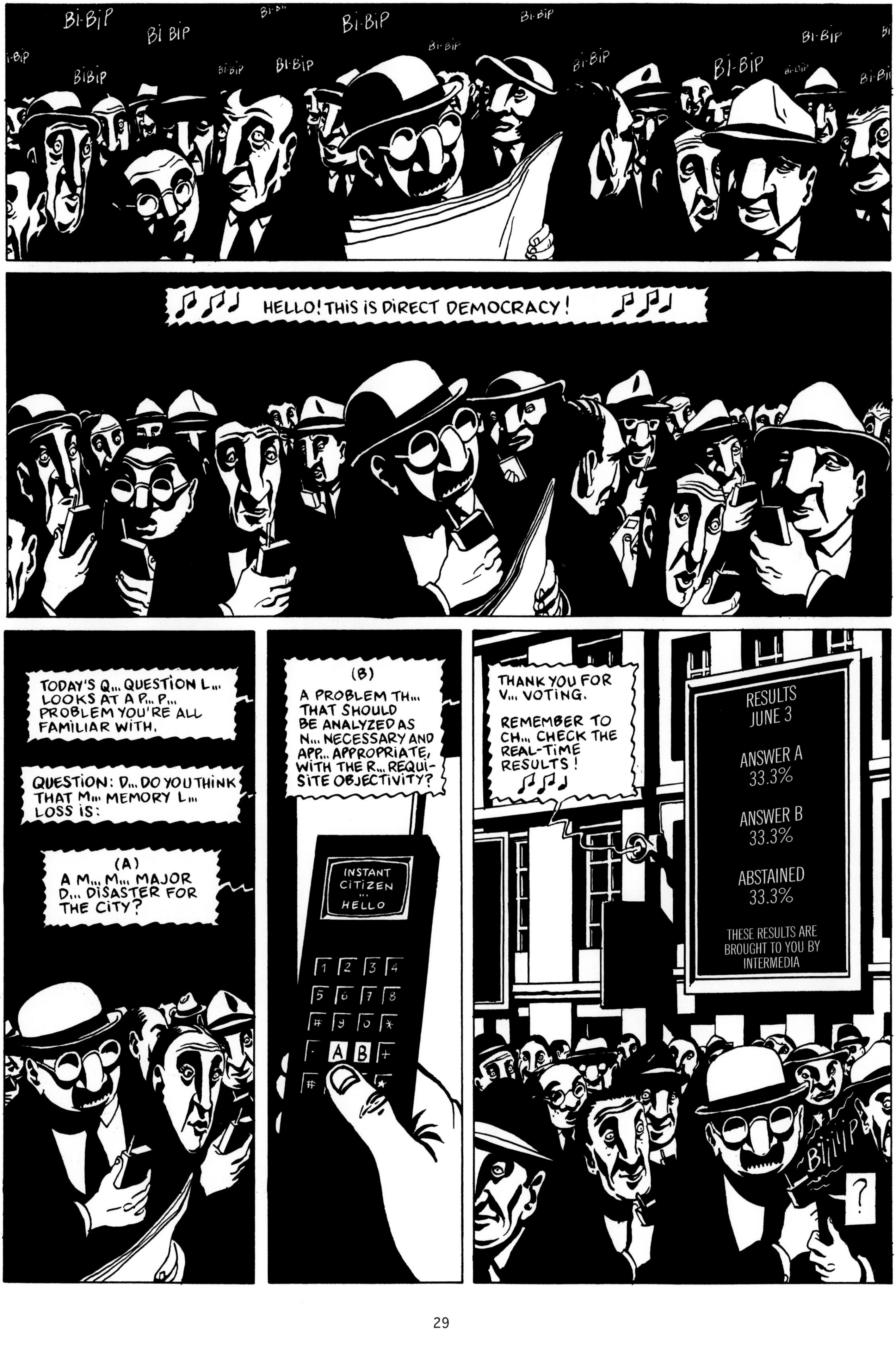

Bi-Bip
Bi Bip
Bi-Bip
Bi-Bip
BiBip
Bi-Bip
Bi-Bip
Bi-Bip
Bi-Bip
Bi-Bip
HELLO! THIS IS DIRECT DEMOCRACY!
TODAY'S Q... QUESTION L... LOOKS AT A P... P... PROBLEM YOU'RE ALL FAMILIAR WITH.
QUESTION: D... DO YOU THINK THAT M... MEMORY L... LOSS IS:
(A) A M... M... MAJOR D... DISASTER FOR THE CITY?
(B) A PROBLEM TH... THAT SHOULD BE ANALYZED AS N... NECESSARY AND APP... APPROPRIATE, WITH THE R... REQUISITE OBJECTIVITY?
INSTANT CITIZEN ... HELLO
1 2 3 4
5 6 7 8
A B
THANK YOU FOR V... VOTING.
REMEMBER TO CH... CHECK THE REAL-TIME RESULTS!
RESULTS
JUNE 3
ANSWER A
33.3%
ANSWER B
33.3%
ABSTAINED
33.3%
THESE RESULTS ARE BROUGHT TO YOU BY INTERMEDIA
Bi-Bip
?

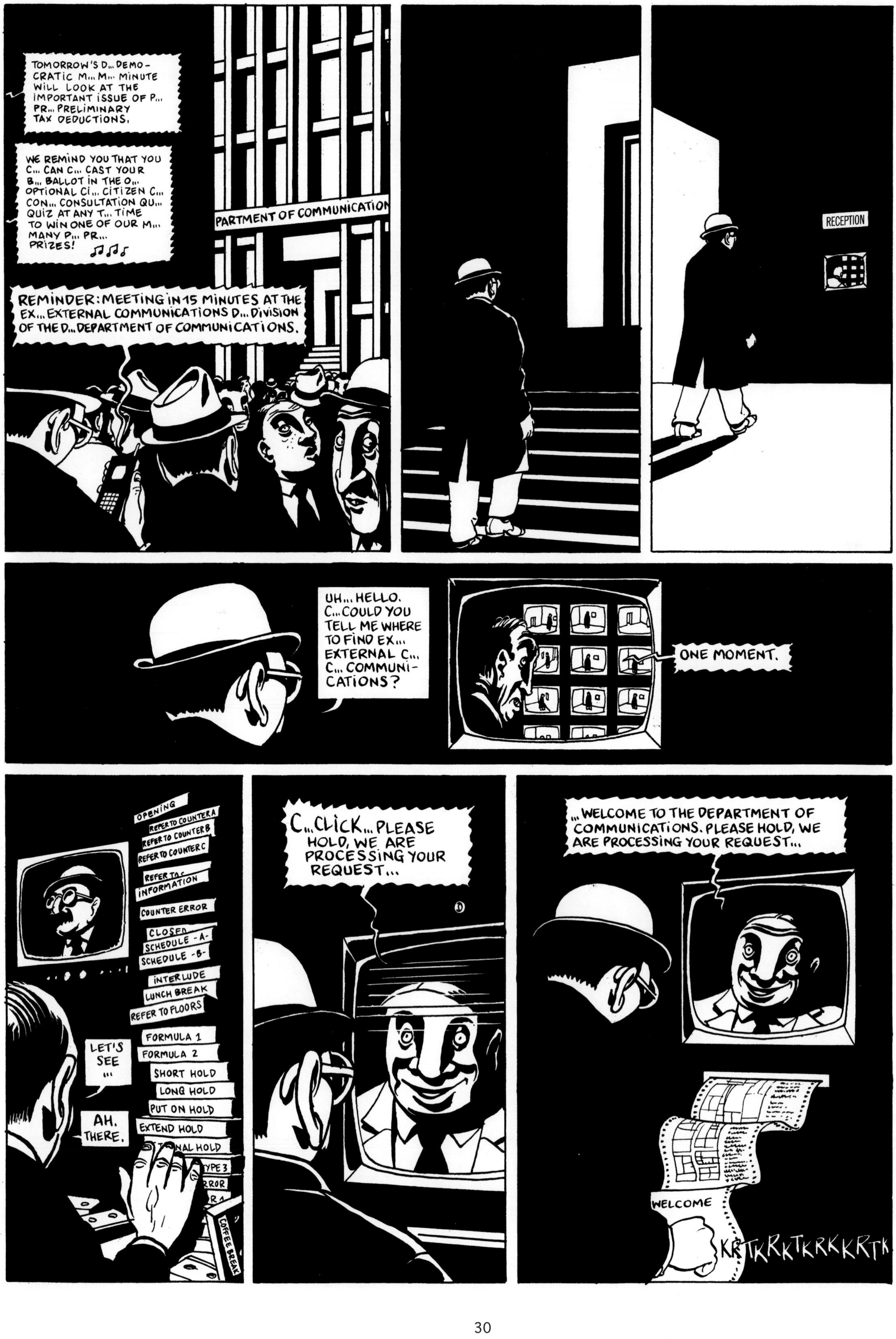
TOMORROW'S D... DEMOCRATIC M... M... MINUTE WILL LOOK AT THE IMPORTANT ISSUE OF P... PR... PRELIMINARY TAX DEDUCTIONS.
WE REMIND YOU THAT YOU C... CAN C... CAST YOUR B... BALLOT IN THE O... OPTIONAL CI... CITIZEN C... CON... CONSULTATION QU... QUIZ AT ANY T... TIME TO WIN ONE OF OUR M... MANY P... PR... PRIZES! ♫♫♫
PARTMENT OF COMMUNICATION
REMINDER: MEETING IN 15 MINUTES AT THE EX... EXTERNAL COMMUNICATIONS D... DIVISION OF THE D... DEPARTMENT OF COMMUNICATIONS.
RECEPTION
UH... HELLO. C... COULD YOU TELL ME WHERE TO FIND EX... EXTERNAL C... C... COMMUNICATIONS?
ONE MOMENT.
OPENING
REFER TO COUNTER A
REFER TO COUNTER B
REFER TO COUNTER C
INFORMATION
COUNTER ERROR
CLOSED
SCHEDULE -A-
SCHEDULE -B-
INTERLUDE
LUNCH BREAK
REFER TO FLOORS
FORMULA 1
FORMULA 2
SHORT HOLD
LONG HOLD
PUT ON HOLD
EXTEND HOLD
COFFEE BREAK
LET'S SEE ...
AH. THERE.
C... CLICK... PLEASE HOLD, WE ARE PROCESSING YOUR REQUEST...
... WELCOME TO THE DEPARTMENT OF COMMUNICATIONS. PLEASE HOLD, WE ARE PROCESSING YOUR REQUEST...
WELCOME
KRTKRKTKRKKRTK

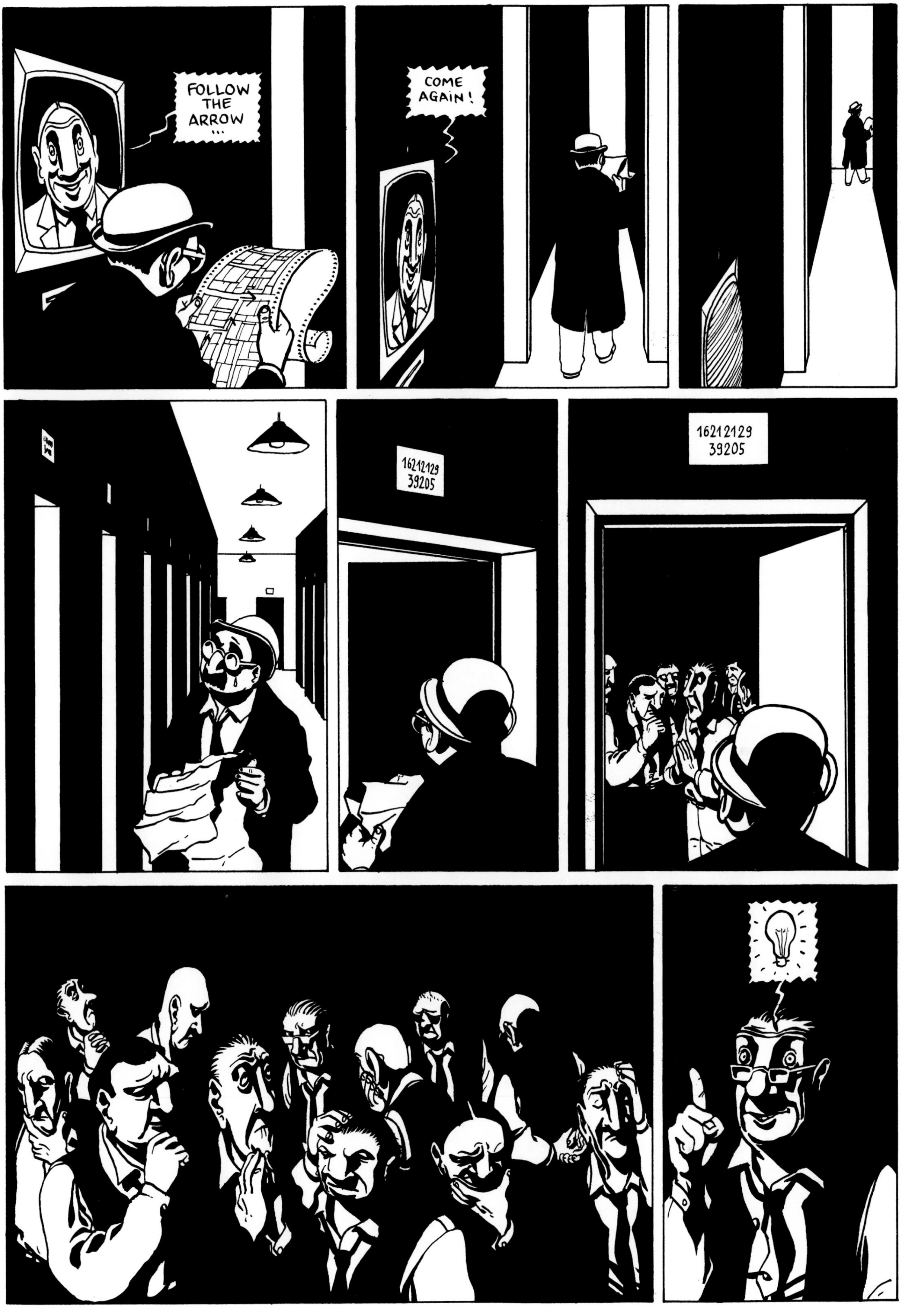
FOLLOW THE ARROW ...
COME AGAIN !
16212129 39205
16212129 39205

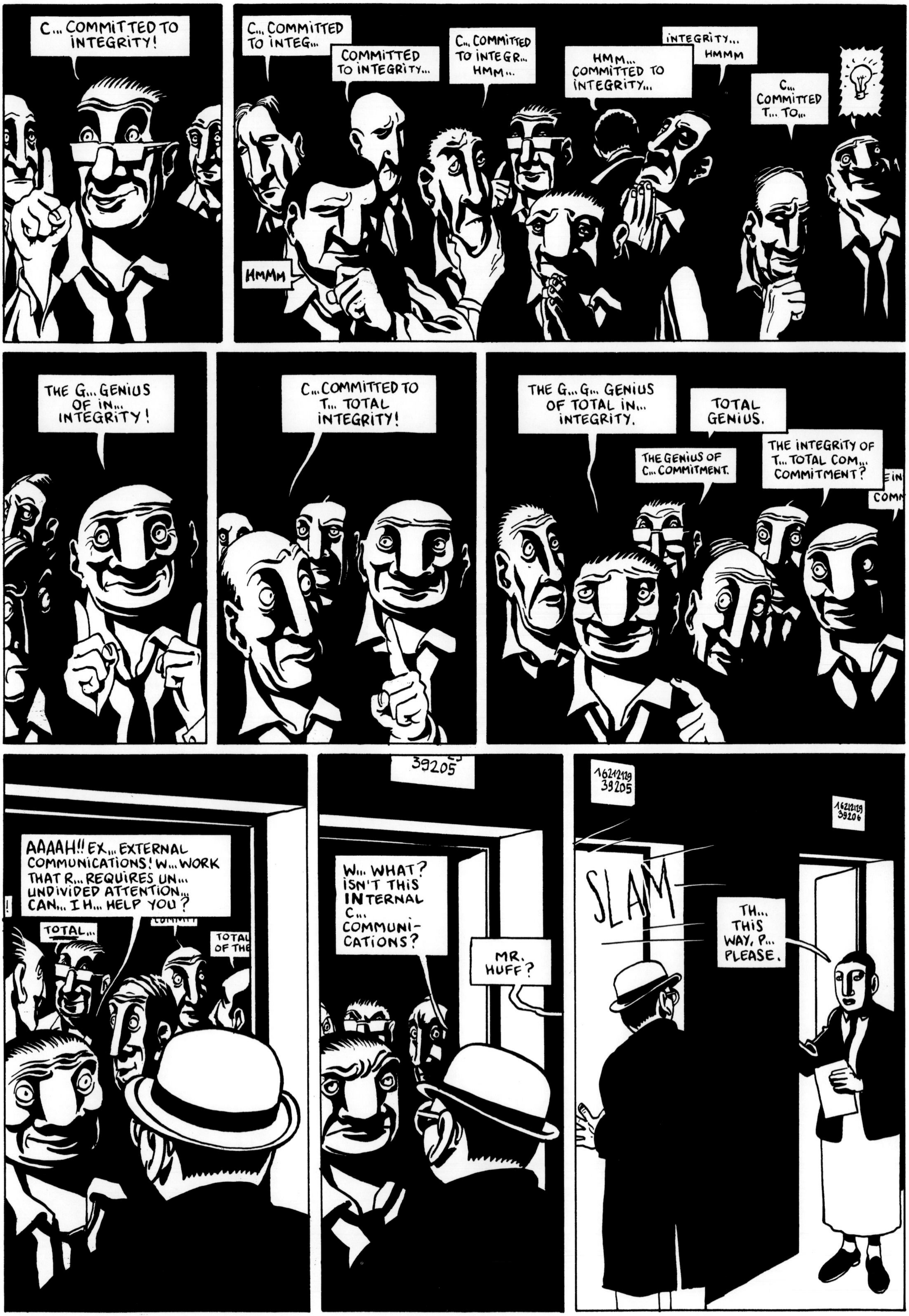
C... COMMITTED TO INTEGRITY!
C... COMMITTED TO INTEG...
COMMITTED TO INTEGRITY...
C... COMMITTED TO INTEGR... HMM...
HMM... COMMITTED TO INTEGRITY...
INTEGRITY... HMMM
C... COMMITTED T... TO...
HMMM
THE G... GENIUS OF IN... INTEGRITY!
C... COMMITTED TO T... TOTAL INTEGRITY!
THE G... G... GENIUS OF TOTAL IN... INTEGRITY.
TOTAL GENIUS.
THE GENIUS OF C... COMMITMENT.
THE INTEGRITY OF T... TOTAL COM... COMMITMENT?
39205
AAAAH!! EX... EXTERNAL COMMUNICATIONS! W... WORK THAT R... REQUIRES UN... UNDIVIDED ATTENTION... CAN... I H... HELP YOU?
TOTAL...
W... WHAT? ISN'T THIS INTERNAL C... COMMUNICATIONS?
MR. HUFF?
16212129 39205
16212129 39206
SLAM
TH... THIS WAY, P... PLEASE.

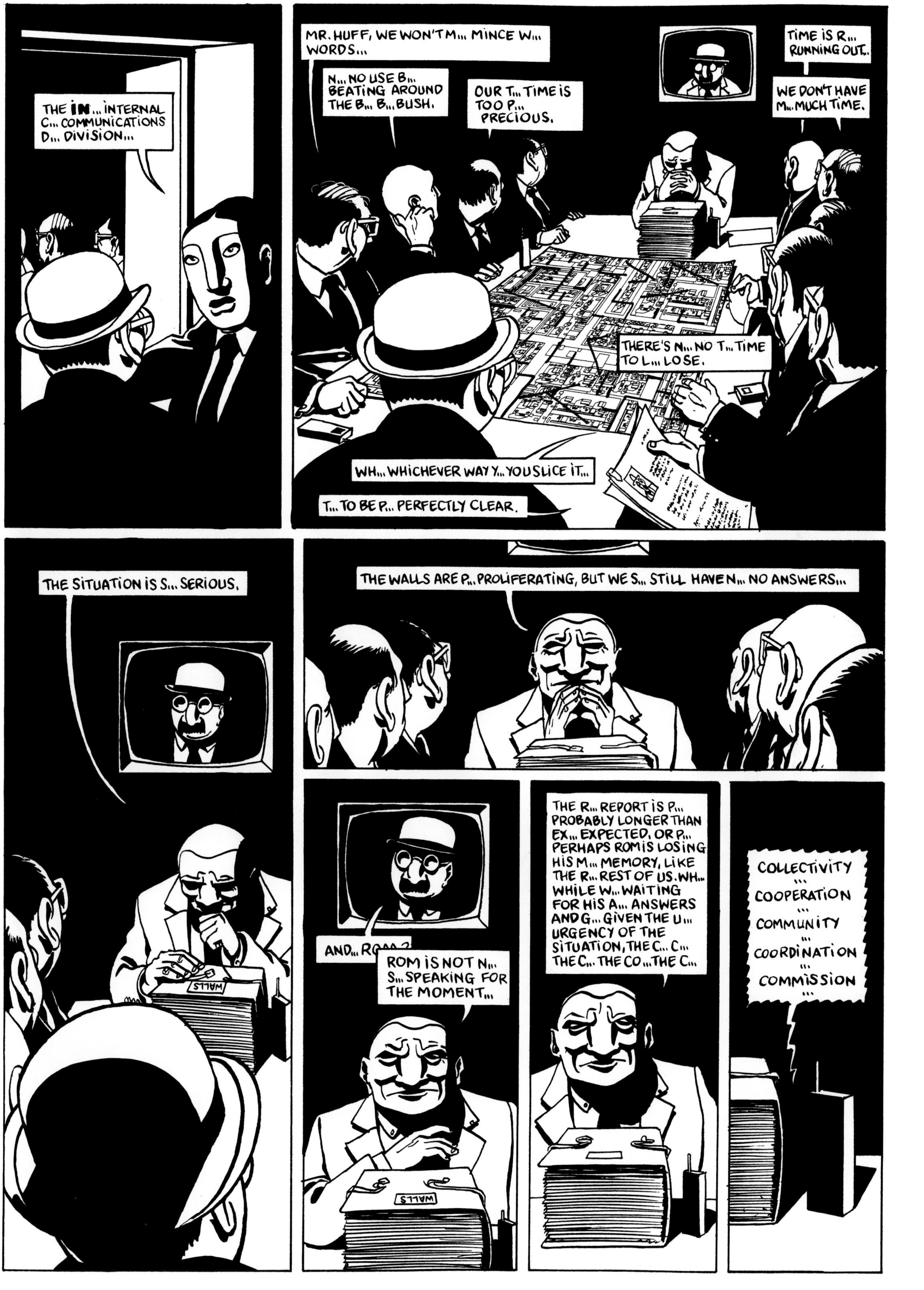
THE IN... INTERNAL C... COMMUNICATIONS D... DIVISION...
MR. HUFF, WE WON'T M... MINCE W... WORDS...
N... NO USE B... BEATING AROUND THE B... B... BUSH.
OUR T... TIME IS TOO P... PRECIOUS.
TIME IS R... RUNNING OUT..
WE DON'T HAVE M... MUCH TIME.
THERE'S N... NO T... TIME TO L... LOSE.
WH... WHICHEVER WAY Y... YOU SLICE IT...
T... TO BE P... PERFECTLY CLEAR.
THE SITUATION IS S... SERIOUS.
THE WALLS ARE P... PROLIFERATING, BUT WE S... STILL HAVEN... NO ANSWERS...
WALLS
AND... ROM ?
ROM IS NOT N... S... SPEAKING FOR THE MOMENT...
WALLS
THE R... REPORT IS P... PROBABLY LONGER THAN EX... EXPECTED, OR P... PERHAPS ROM IS LOSING HIS M... MEMORY, LIKE THE R... REST OF US. WH... WHILE W... WAITING FOR HIS A... ANSWERS AND G... GIVEN THE U... URGENCY OF THE SITUATION, THE C... C... THE C... THE CO... THE C...
COLLECTIVITY ... COOPERATION ... COMMUNITY ... COORDINATION ... COMMISSION ...

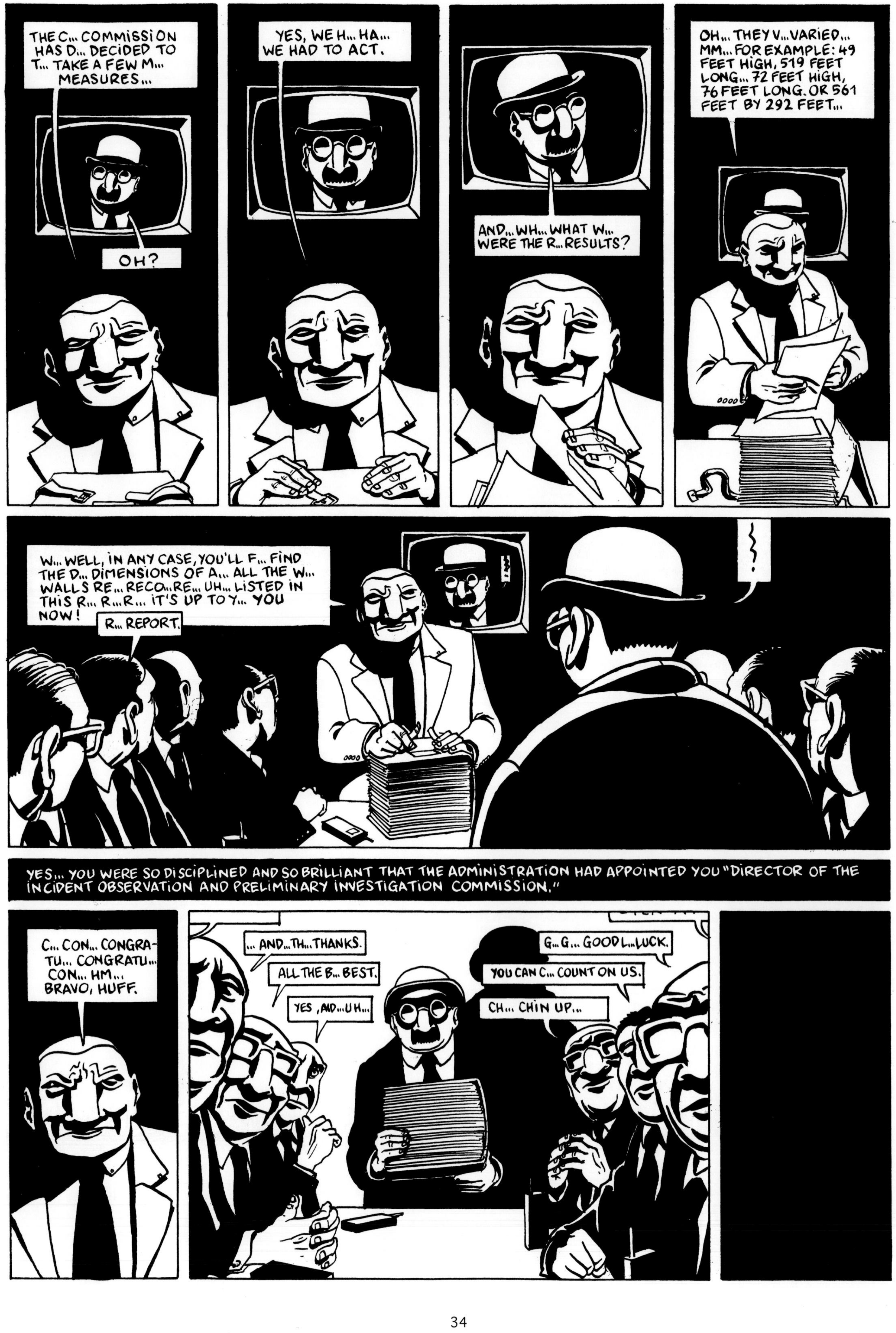
THE C... COMMISSION HAS D... DECIDED TO T... TAKE A FEW M... MEASURES...
OH?
YES, WE H... HA... WE HAD TO ACT.
AND... WH... WHAT W... WERE THE R... RESULTS?
OH... THEY V... VARIED... MM... FOR EXAMPLE: 49 FEET HIGH, 519 FEET LONG... 72 FEET HIGH, 76 FEET LONG. OR 561 FEET BY 292 FEET...
W... WELL, IN ANY CASE, YOU'LL F... FIND THE D... DIMENSIONS OF A... ALL THE W... WALLS RE... RECO... RE... UH... LISTED IN THIS R... R... R... IT'S UP TO Y... YOU NOW!
R... REPORT.
YES... YOU WERE SO DISCIPLINED AND SO BRILLIANT THAT THE ADMINISTRATION HAD APPOINTED YOU "DIRECTOR OF THE INCIDENT OBSERVATION AND PRELIMINARY INVESTIGATION COMMISSION."
C... CON... CONGRA-TU... CONGRATU... CON... HM... BRAVO, HUFF.
... AND... TH... THANKS.
ALL THE B... BEST.
YES, AND... UH...
G... G... GOOD L... LUCK.
YOU CAN C... COUNT ON US.
CH... CHIN UP...

CHAPTER 5

DEAD END

(00424)

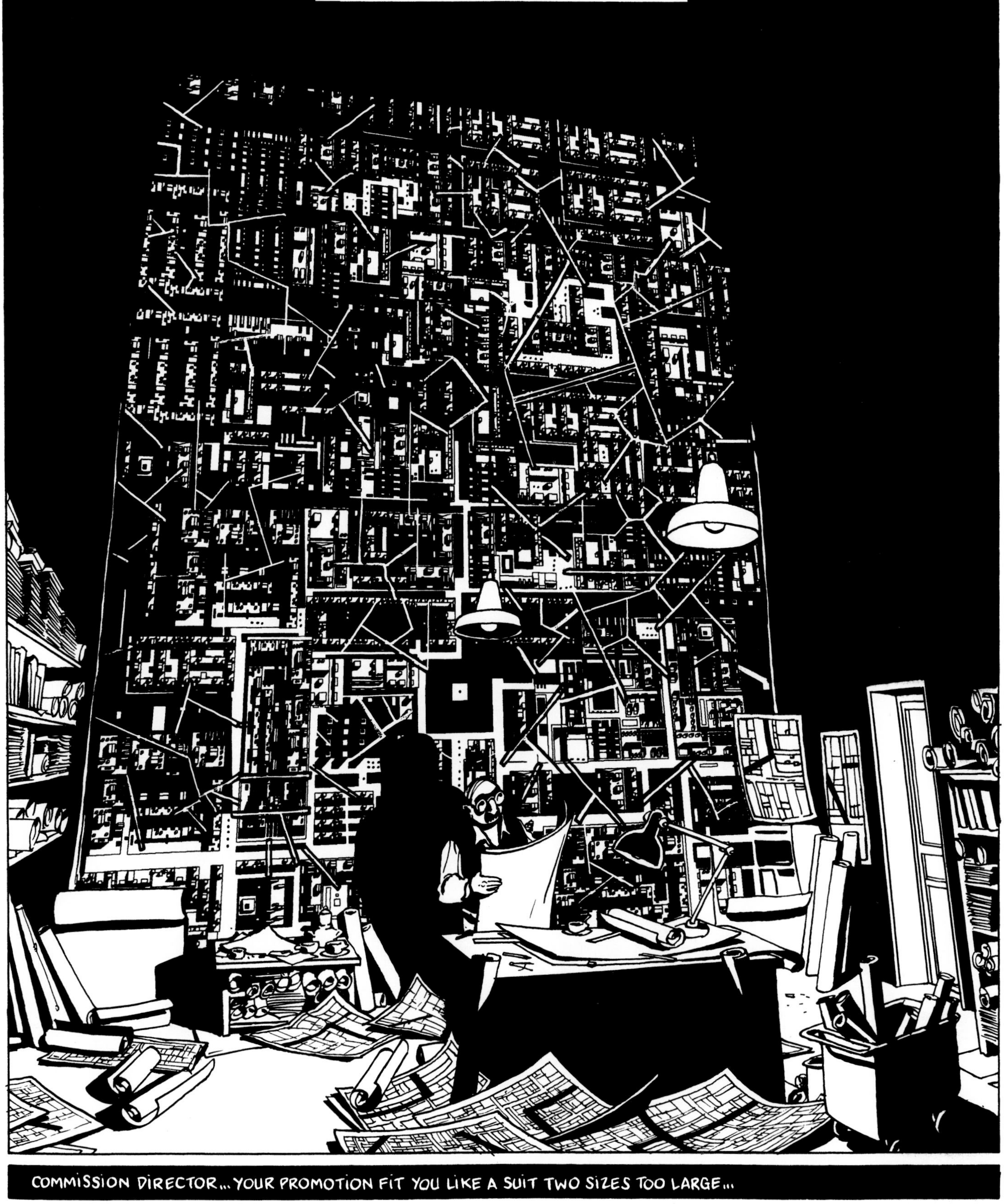

COMMISSION DIRECTOR... YOUR PROMOTION FIT YOU LIKE A SUIT TWO SIZES TOO LARGE...

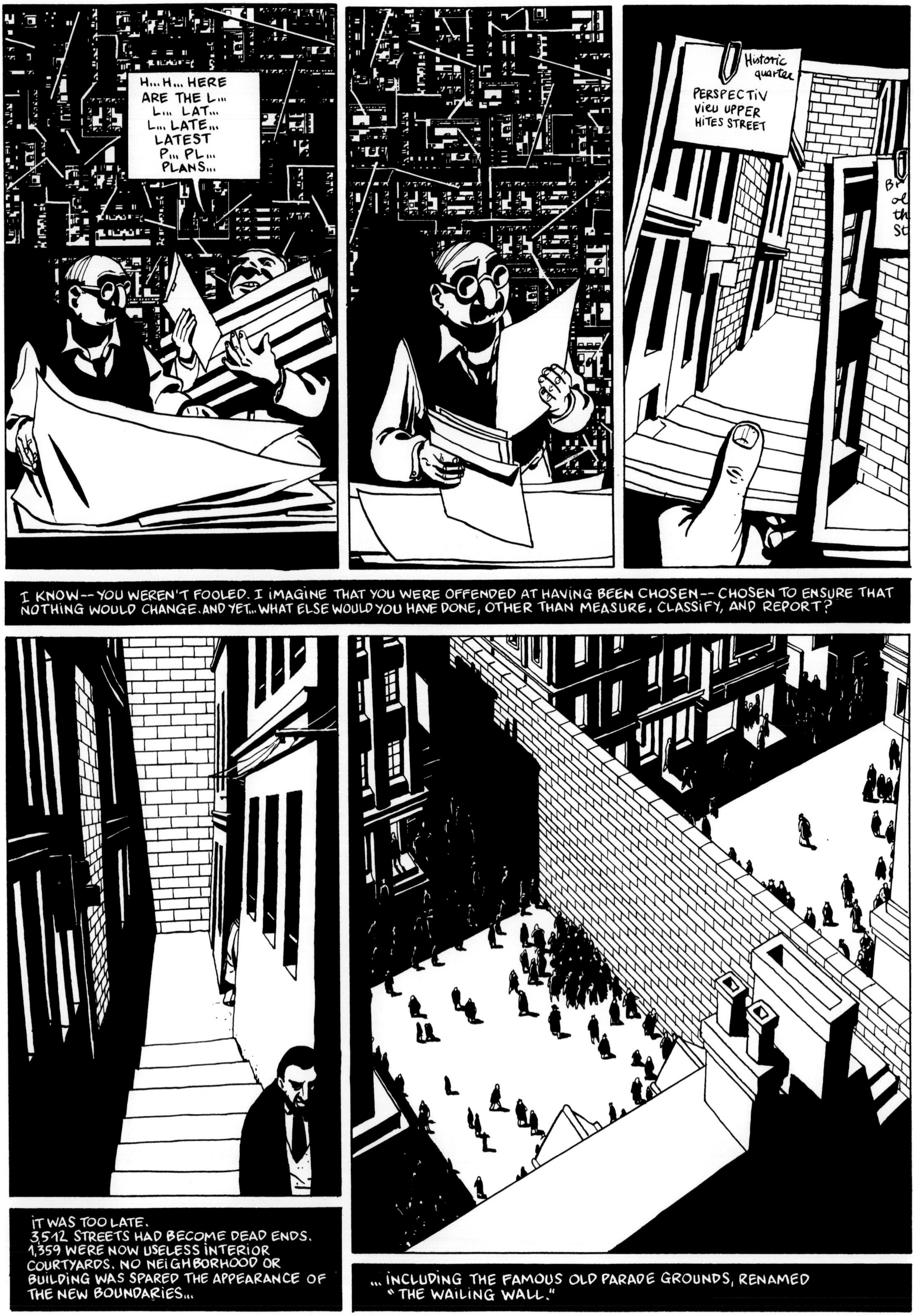
H... H... HERE ARE THE L... L... LAT... L... LATE... LATEST P... PL... PLANS...
Historic quarter
PERSPECTIV vieu UPPER HITES STREET
I KNOW--YOU WEREN'T FOOLED. I IMAGINE THAT YOU WERE OFFENDED AT HAVING BEEN CHOSEN--CHOSEN TO ENSURE THAT NOTHING WOULD CHANGE. AND YET... WHAT ELSE WOULD YOU HAVE DONE, OTHER THAN MEASURE, CLASSIFY, AND REPORT?
IT WAS TOO LATE. 3,512 STREETS HAD BECOME DEAD ENDS. 1,359 WERE NOW USELESS INTERIOR COURTYARDS. NO NEIGHBORHOOD OR BUILDING WAS SPARED THE APPEARANCE OF THE NEW BOUNDARIES...
... INCLUDING THE FAMOUS OLD PARADE GROUNDS, RENAMED "THE WAILING WALL."

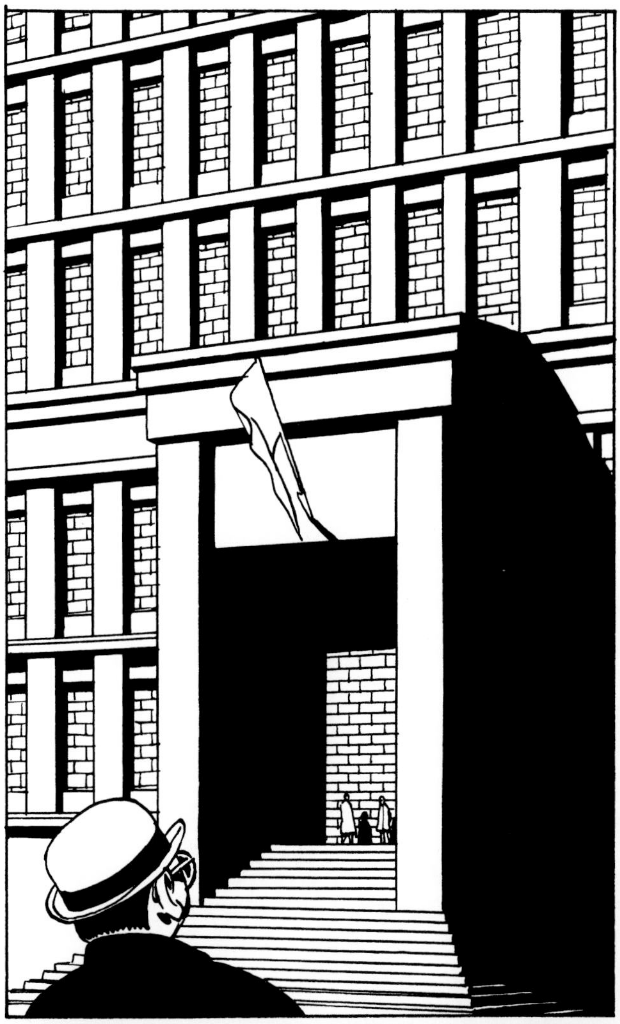

THE MINISTRY OF JUSTICE PROCLAIMED ITS SELF-DETERMINATION. THE FEW LAWS IT MANAGED TO ENACT, DESPITE THE AMNESIA OF THE LAWMAKERS, APPLIED ONLY TO THE MINISTRY ITSELF...

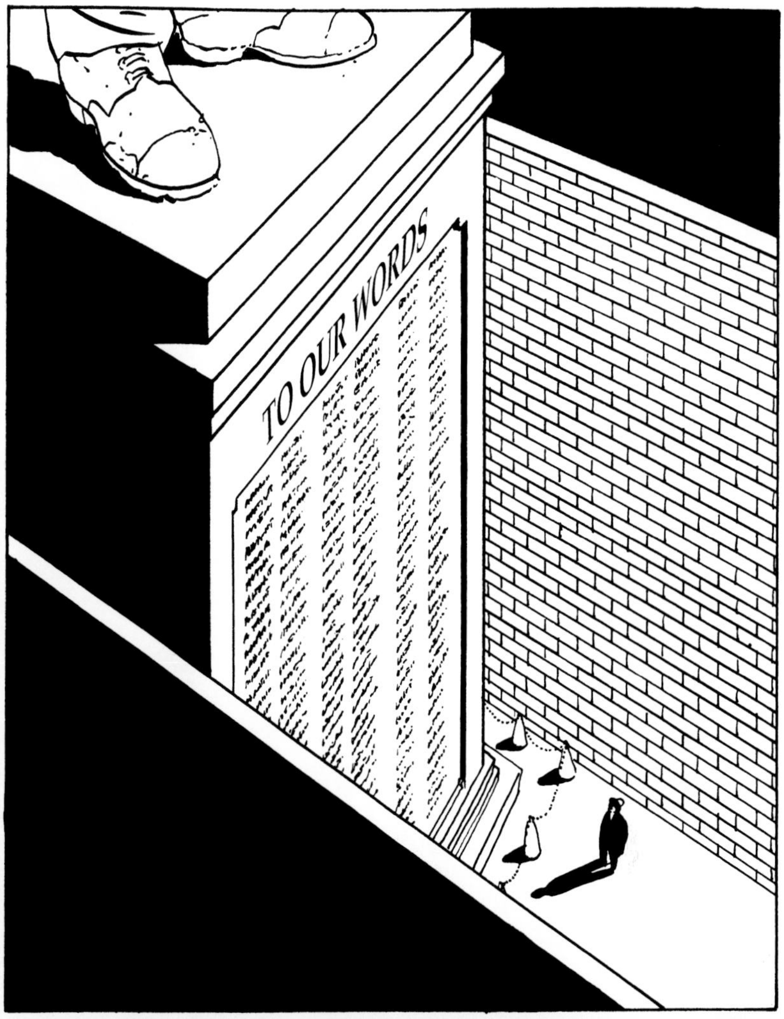
TO OUR WORDS

AND FOLLOWING A COMPLICATED SERIES OF EVENTS, THE WORDS MONUMENT FOUND ITSELF CORNERED IN A NO MAN'S LAND. THE MEMORY OF WORDS, TRAPPED IN A RESTRICTED ZONE -- FACT IS SOMETIMES STRANGER THAN FICTION...

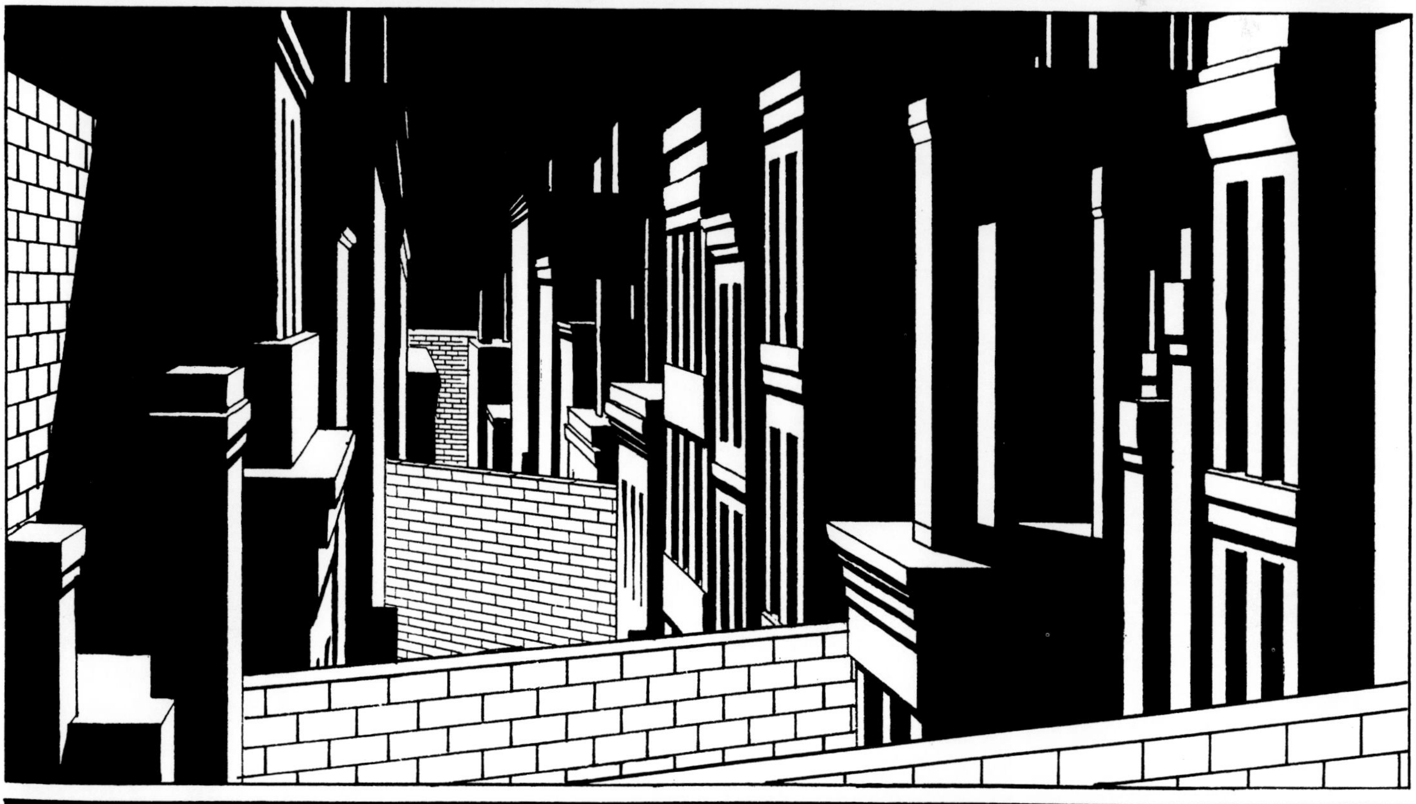

THE WALLS HAD CRYSTALLIZED THE CITY. THERE REMAINED ONLY TWO KINDS OF PEOPLE: THOSE WHO BUILT WALLS, AND THOSE TRYING TO FIND AN UNLIKELY PATH THROUGH THE LABYRINTH OF STREETS AND BLIND ALLEYS.

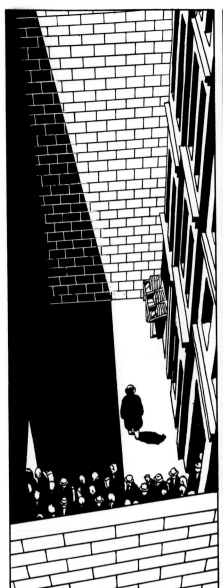

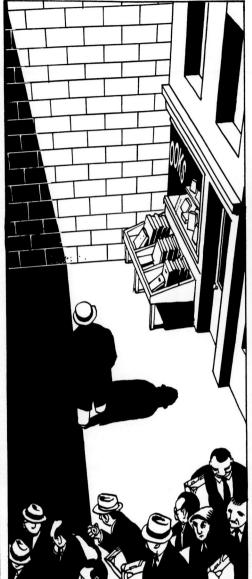

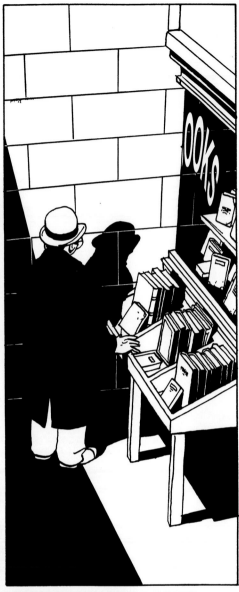

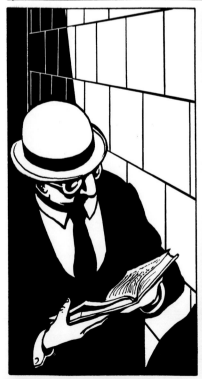

OOKS
NNECTION
E-CONNECTION
THAT DAY, YOU COUNTED ALL THE WORDS YOU STILL KNEW: 424.

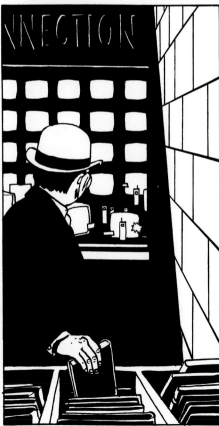

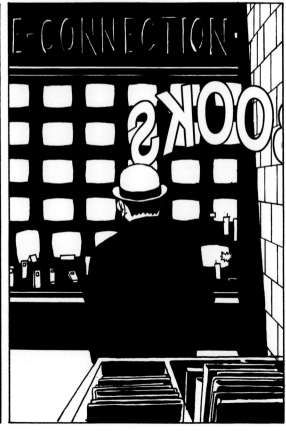

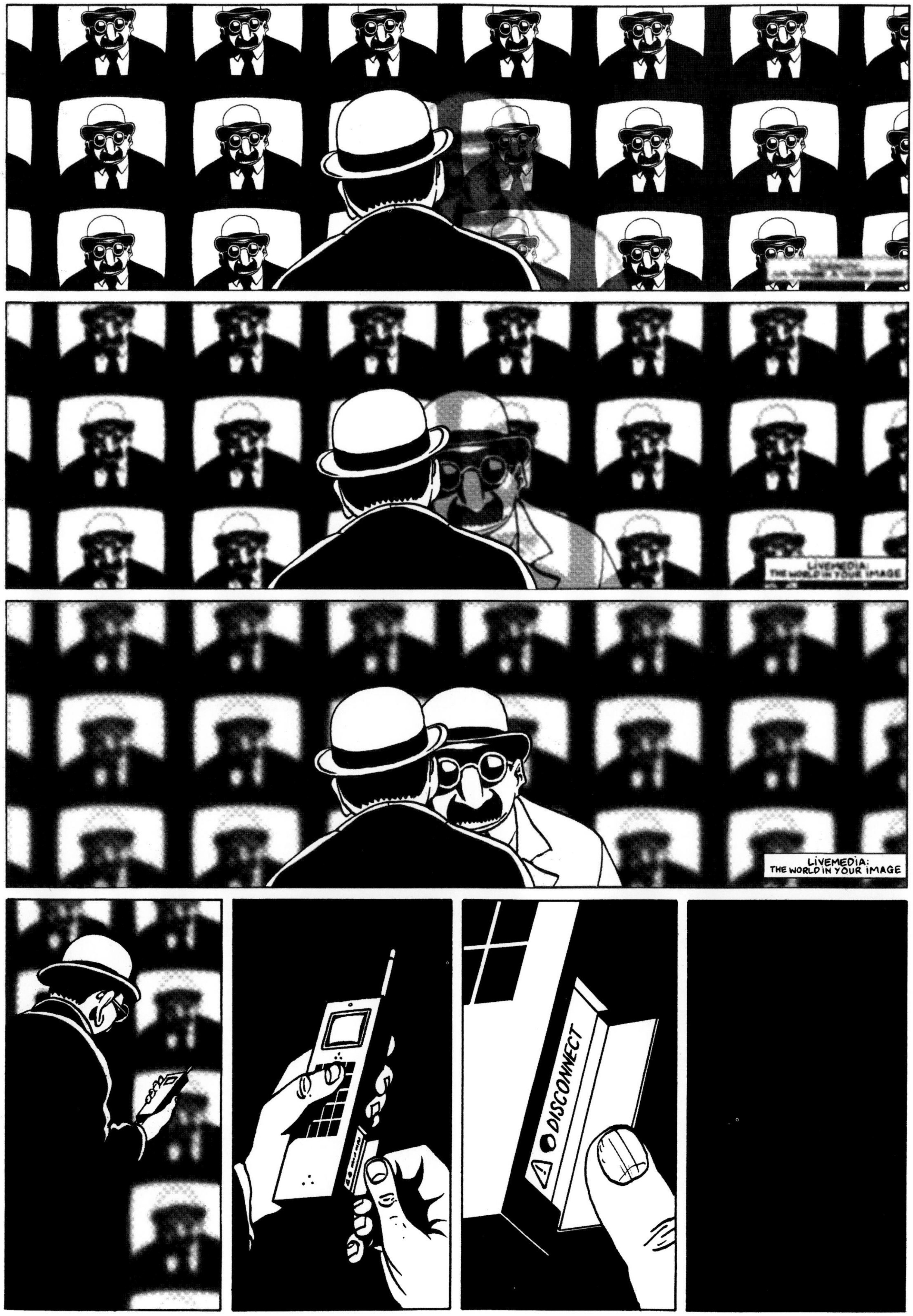
LIVEMEDIA:
THE WORLD IN YOUR IMAGE
LIVEMEDIA:
THE WORLD IN YOUR IMAGE
DISCONNECT

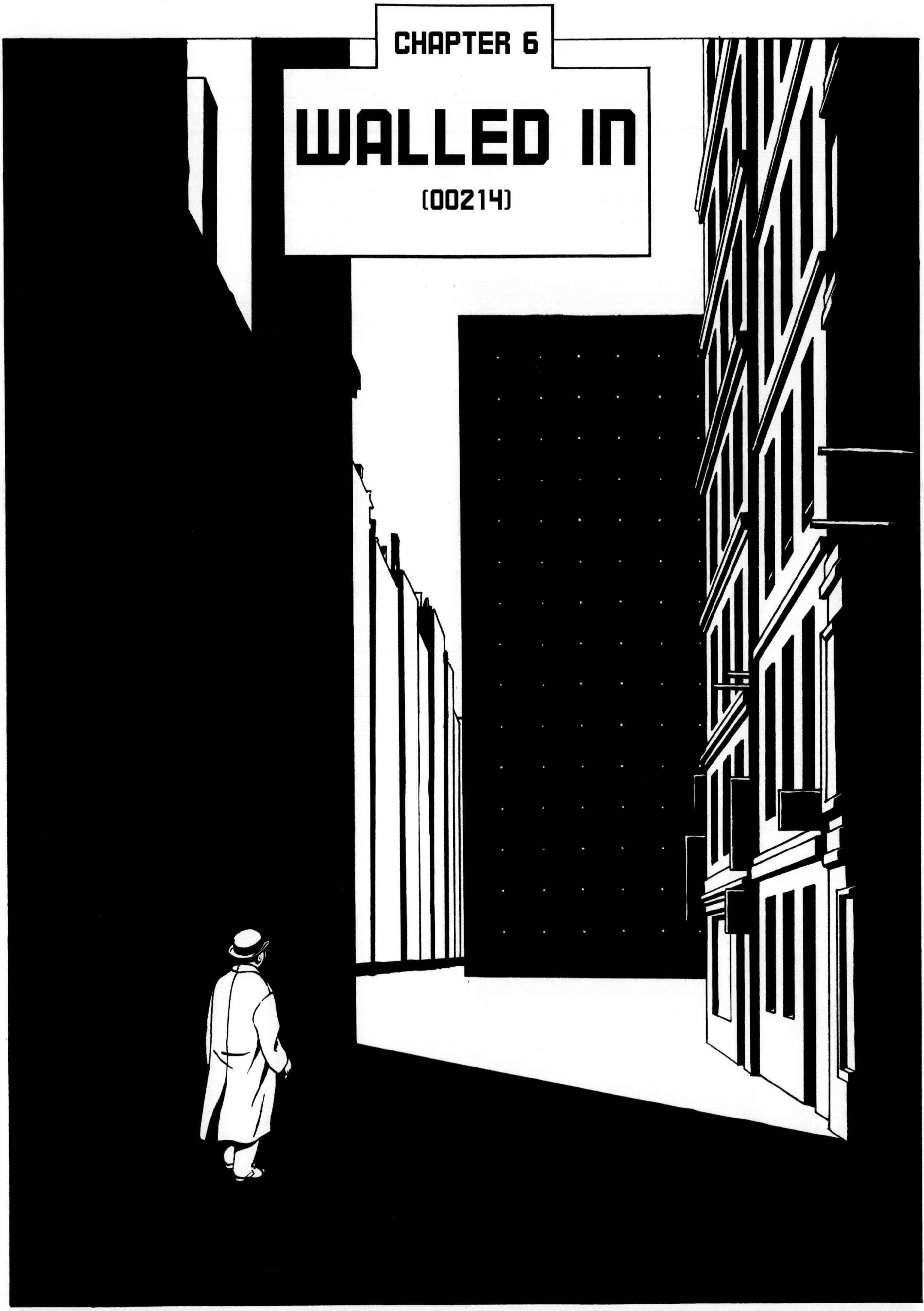
CHAPTER 6
WALLED IN
(00214)

THAT NIGHT, YOU HAD A DREAM... THE CITY WAS PLUNGED IN SHADOW... THE STREETS WERE SILENT AND STRANGELY EMPTY...

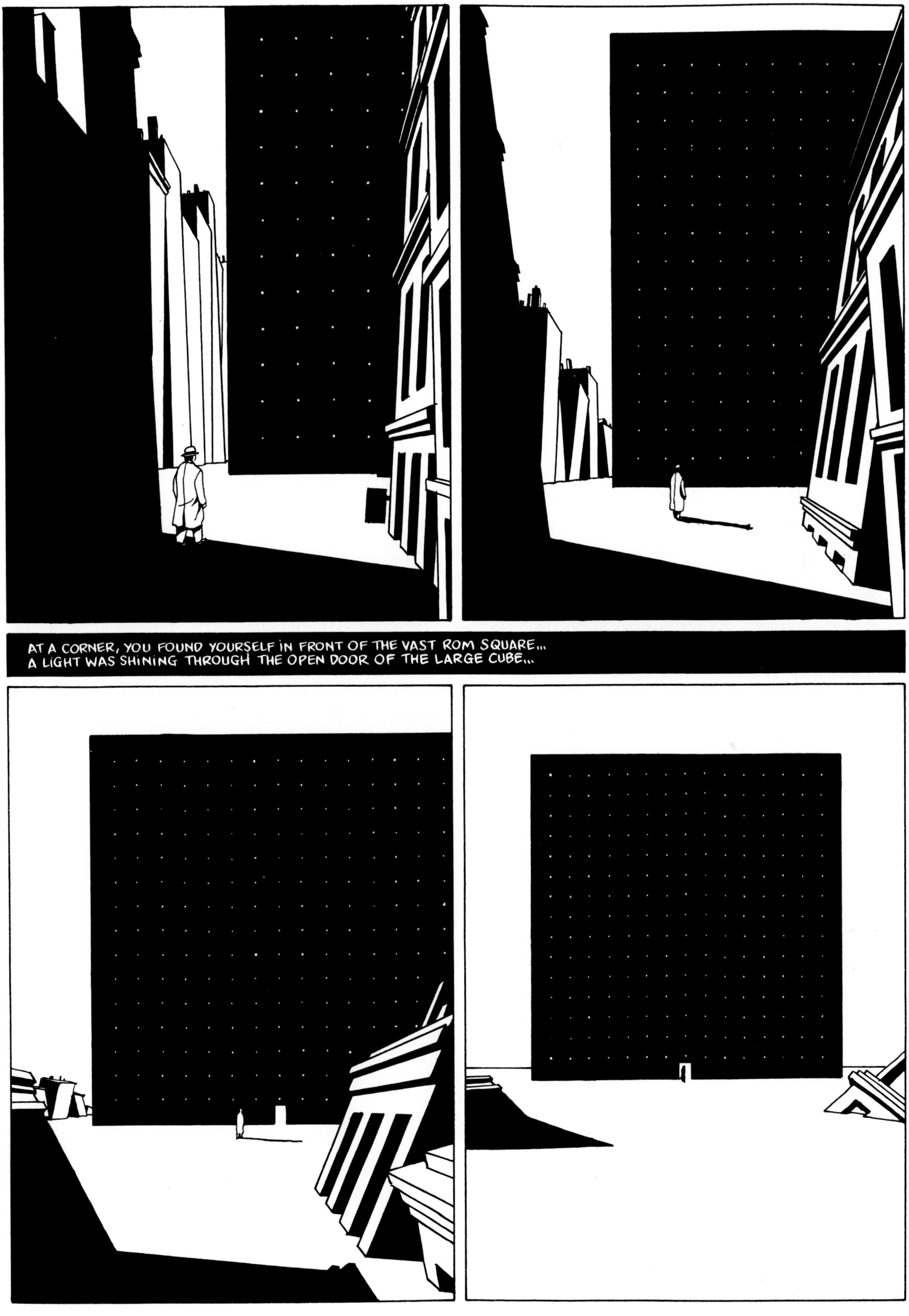
AT A CORNER, YOU FOUND YOURSELF IN FRONT OF THE VAST ROM SQUARE...
A LIGHT WAS SHINING THROUGH THE OPEN DOOR OF THE LARGE CUBE...

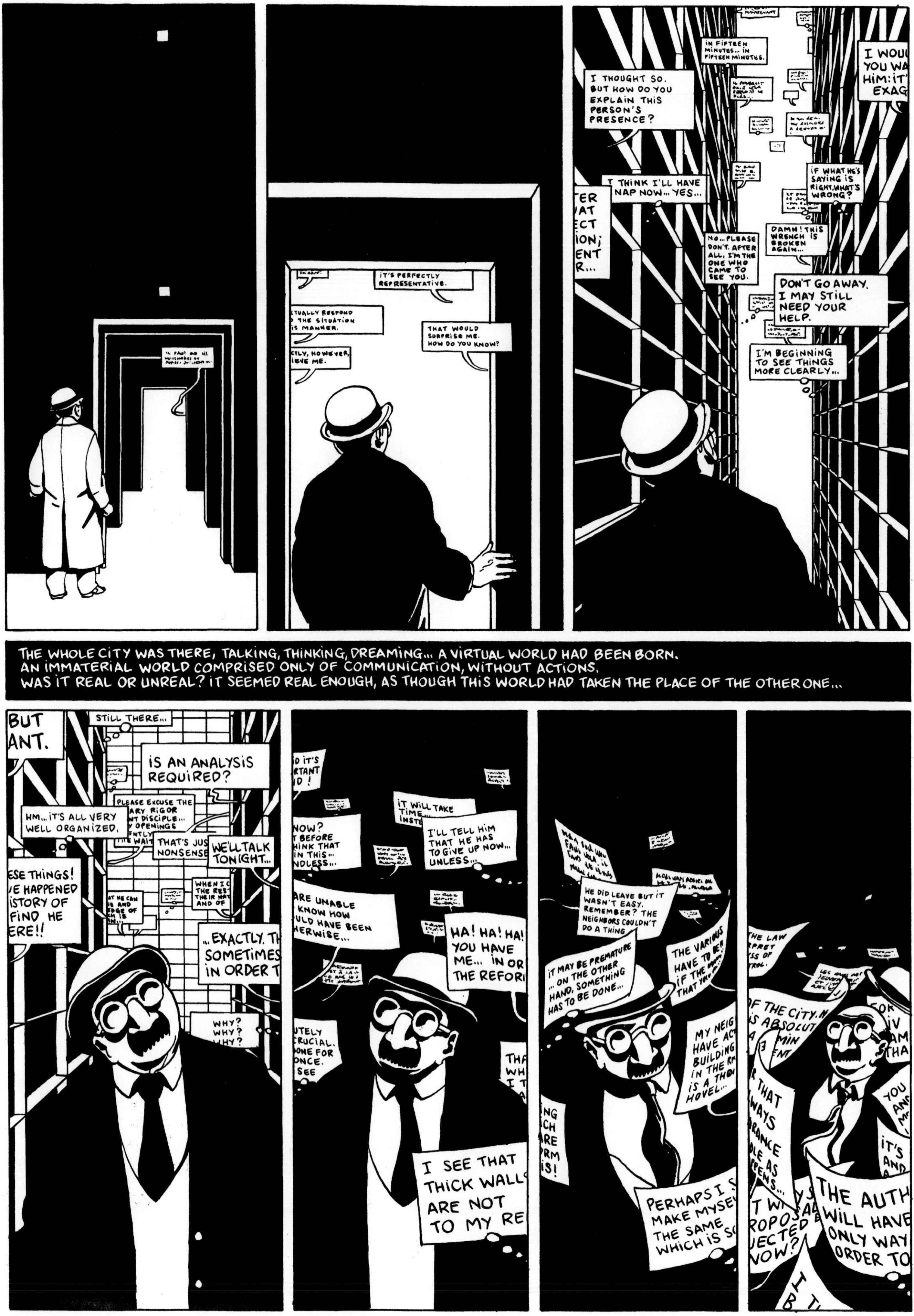
IT'S PERFECTLY REPRESENTATIVE.
THAT WOULD SURPRISE ME. HOW DO YOU KNOW?
IN FIFTEEN MINUTES... IN FIFTEEN MINUTES.
I THOUGHT SO. BUT HOW DO YOU EXPLAIN THIS PERSON'S PRESENCE?
I THINK I'LL HAVE NAP NOW... YES...
IF WHAT HE'S SAYING IS RIGHT, WHAT'S WRONG?
DAMN! THIS WRENCH IS BROKEN AGAIN...
NO... PLEASE DON'T. AFTER ALL, I'M THE ONE WHO CAME TO SEE YOU.
DON'T GO AWAY. I MAY STILL NEED YOUR HELP.
I'M BEGINNING TO SEE THINGS MORE CLEARLY...
THE WHOLE CITY WAS THERE, TALKING, THINKING, DREAMING... A VIRTUAL WORLD HAD BEEN BORN.
AN IMMATERIAL WORLD COMPRISED ONLY OF COMMUNICATION, WITHOUT ACTIONS.
WAS IT REAL OR UNREAL? IT SEEMED REAL ENOUGH, AS THOUGH THIS WORLD HAD TAKEN THE PLACE OF THE OTHER ONE...
STILL THERE...
IS AN ANALYSIS REQUIRED?
HM... IT'S ALL VERY WELL ORGANIZED.
THAT'S JUST NONSENSE
WE'LL TALK TONIGHT...
WHY? WHY? WHY?
I'LL TELL HIM THAT HE HAS TO GIVE UP NOW... UNLESS...
HA! HA! HA! YOU HAVE ME...
I SEE THAT THICK WALLS ARE NOT TO MY RE
HE DID LEAVE BUT IT WASN'T EASY. REMEMBER? THE NEIGHBORS COULDN'T DO A THING
IT MAY BE PREMATURE ... ON THE OTHER HAND, SOMETHING HAS TO BE DONE...
PERHAPS I S MAKE MYSE THE SAME WHICH IS S
THE AUTH WILL HAVE ONLY WAY ORDER TO

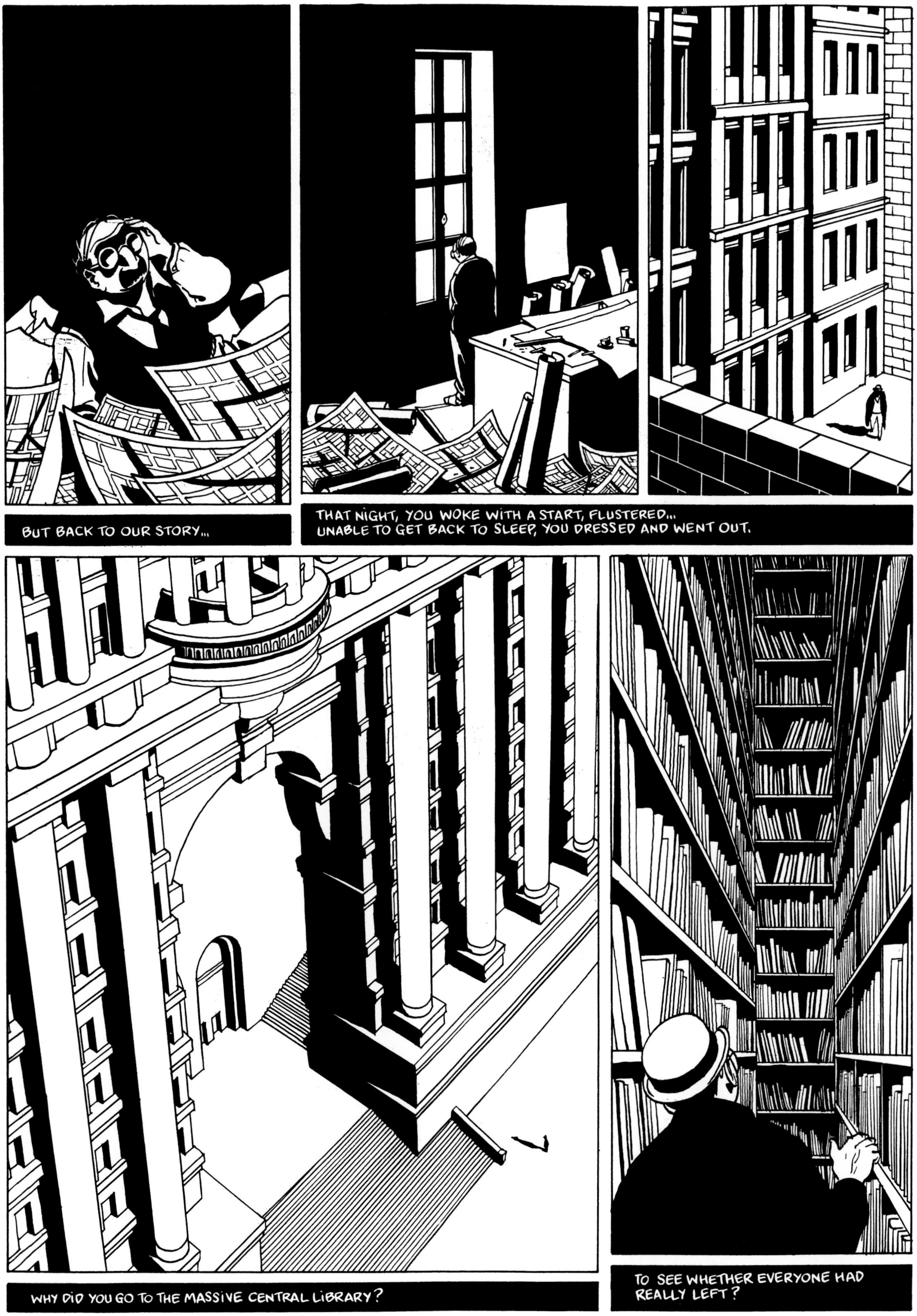
BUT BACK TO OUR STORY...
THAT NIGHT, YOU WOKE WITH A START, FLUSTERED...
UNABLE TO GET BACK TO SLEEP, YOU DRESSED AND WENT OUT.
WHY DID YOU GO TO THE MASSIVE CENTRAL LIBRARY?
TO SEE WHETHER EVERYONE HAD REALLY LEFT?

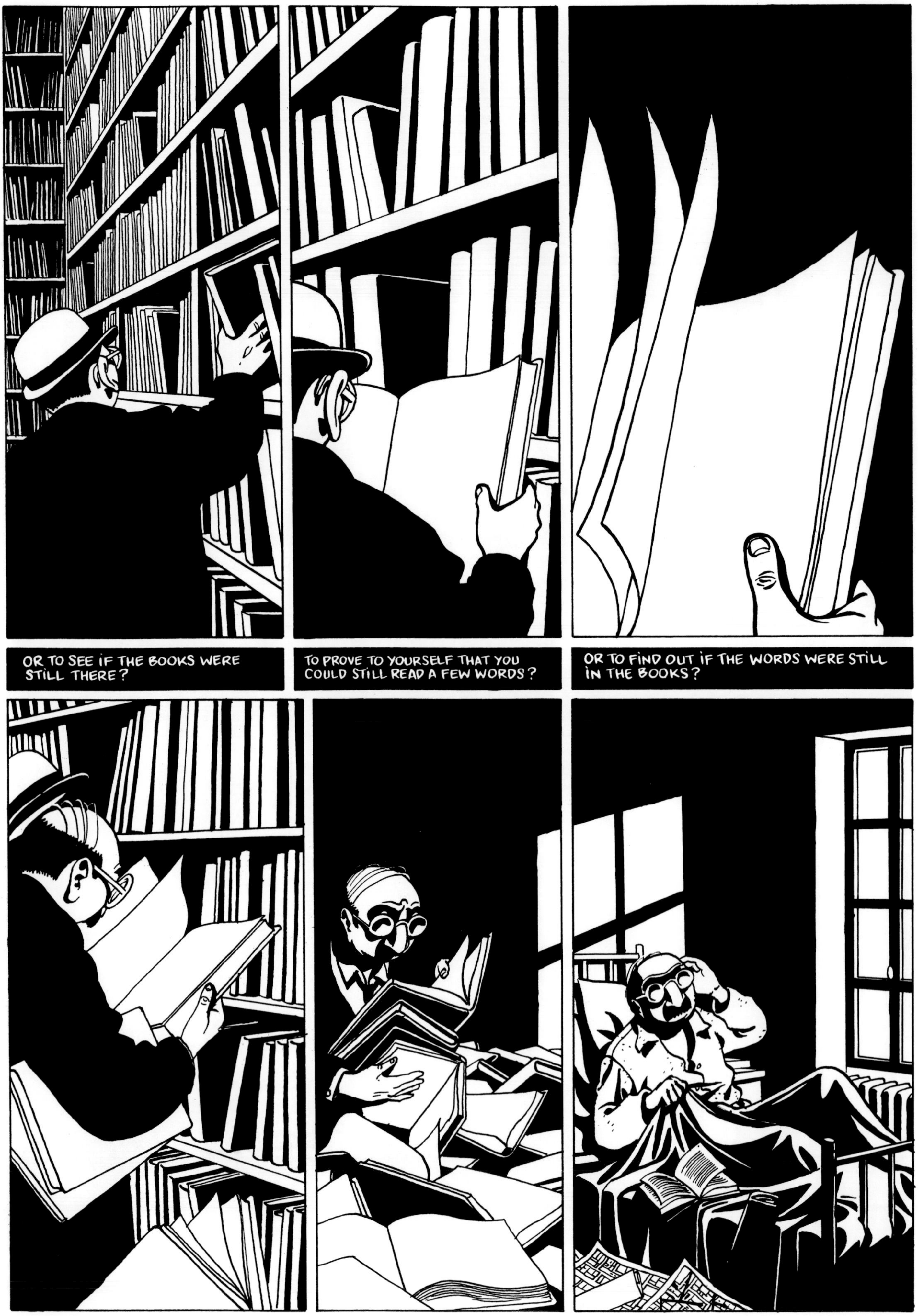
OR TO SEE IF THE BOOKS WERE STILL THERE?
TO PROVE TO YOURSELF THAT YOU COULD STILL READ A FEW WORDS?
OR TO FIND OUT IF THE WORDS WERE STILL IN THE BOOKS?

OUR CITY HAD BECOME LIKE A LONG SHADOW, GRIM AND SILENT. THE EXODUS WAS DWINDLING, AND ITS LAST STRAGGLERS BRUSHED AGAINST THE WALLS...

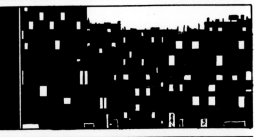

THAT WAS WHEN YOU DECIDED TO COME SEE ME...

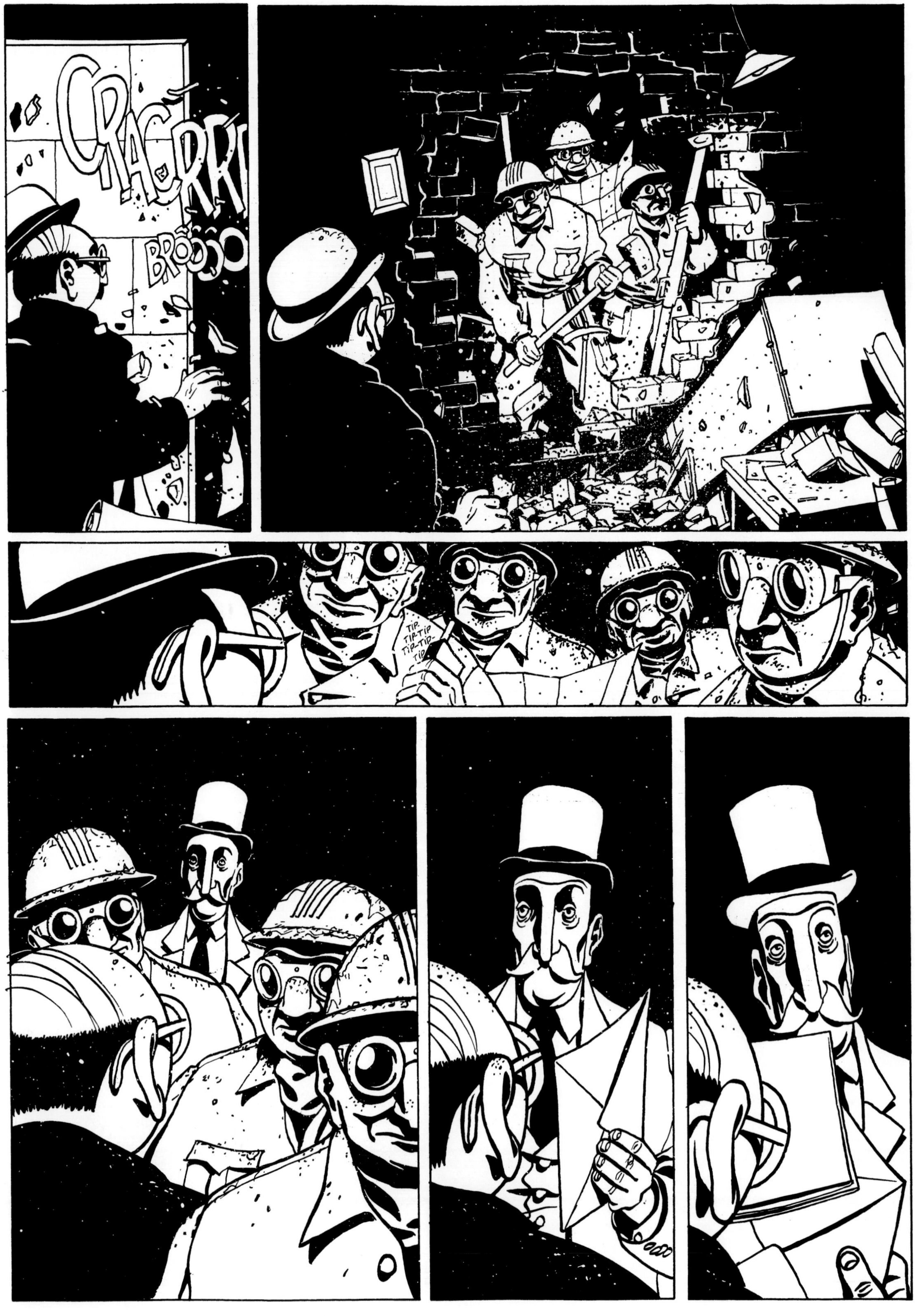
CRACRR
BROOOO
TIP-TIP-TIP-TIP-TIP-TIP

X
CRCKRR
BRÔÔÔÔ

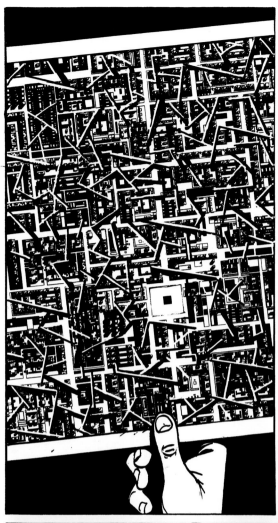

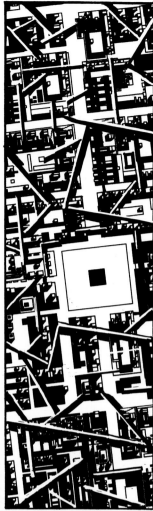

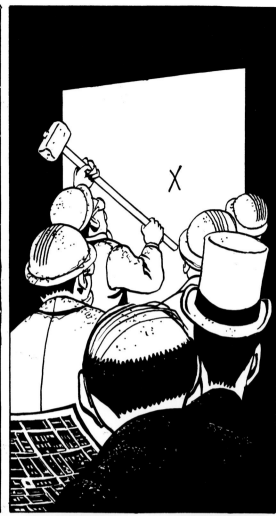

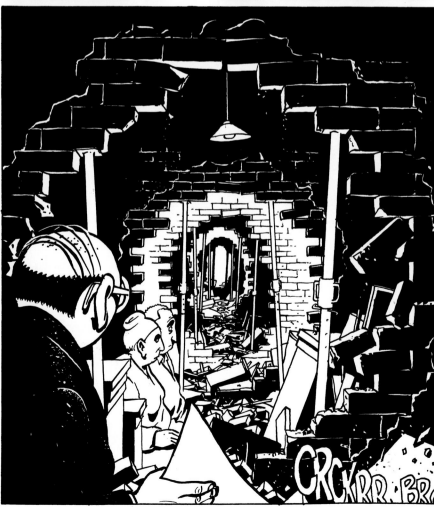

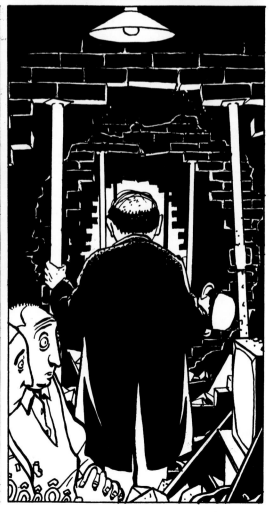

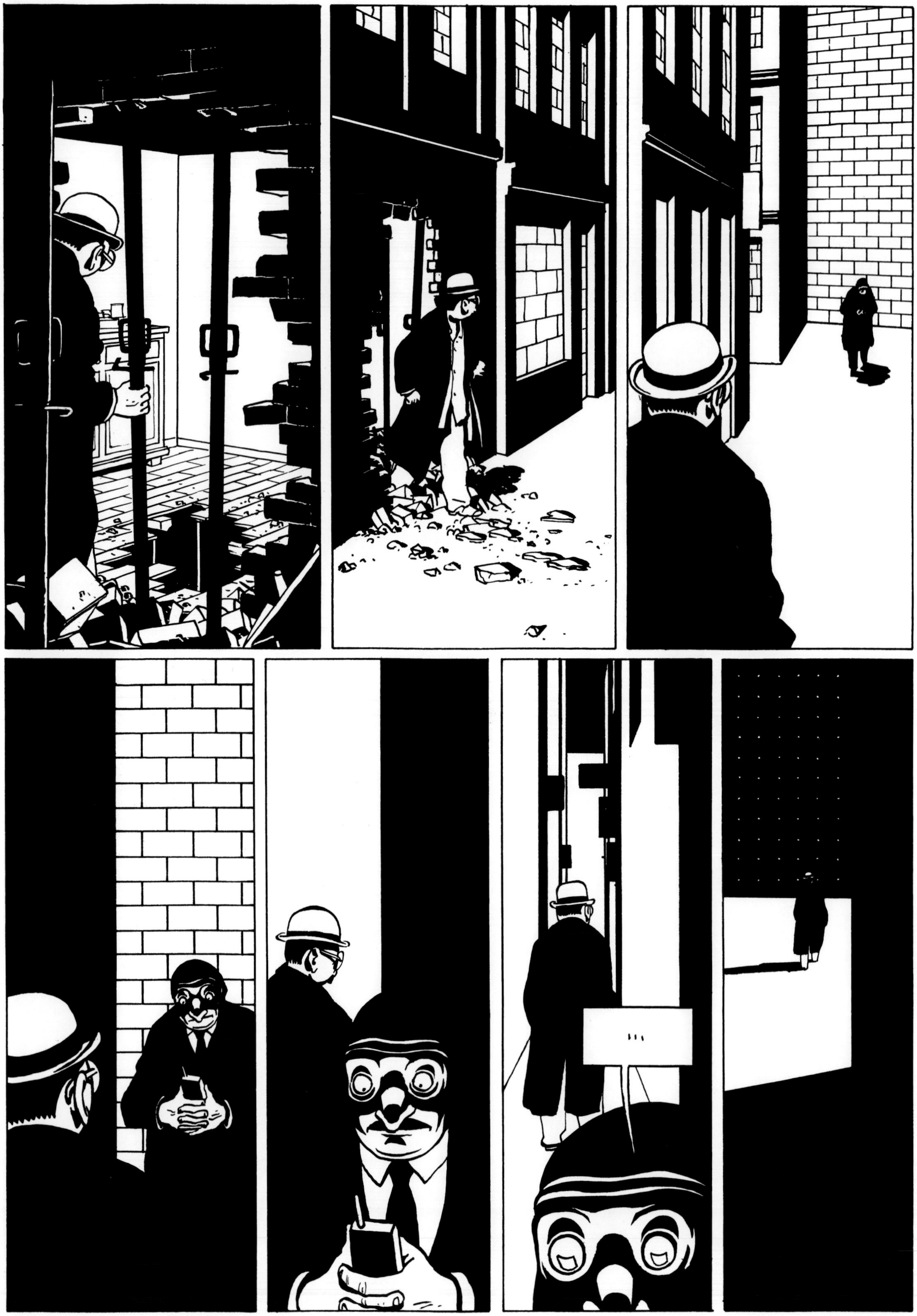

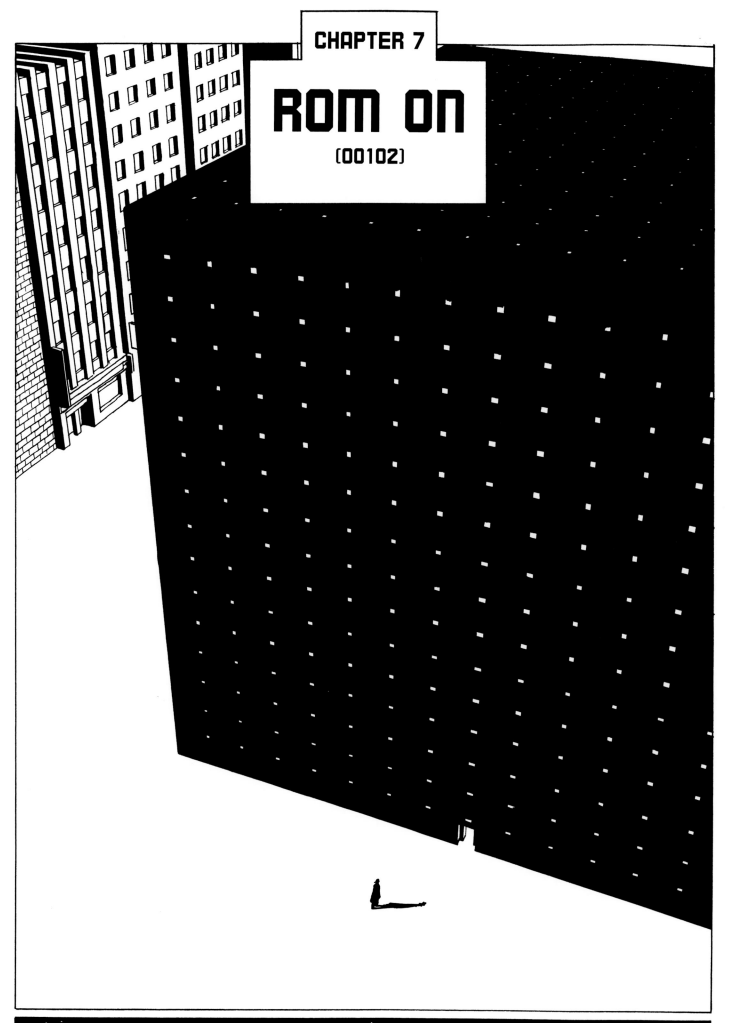

THIS IS THE STORY OF A MONSTER: ROM, BORN OF THE UNLIKELY COMMINGLING OF THE AUDACITY OF DREAMS AND THE INGENUITY OF SCIENCE. (OR WAS IT THE OTHER WAY AROUND?)

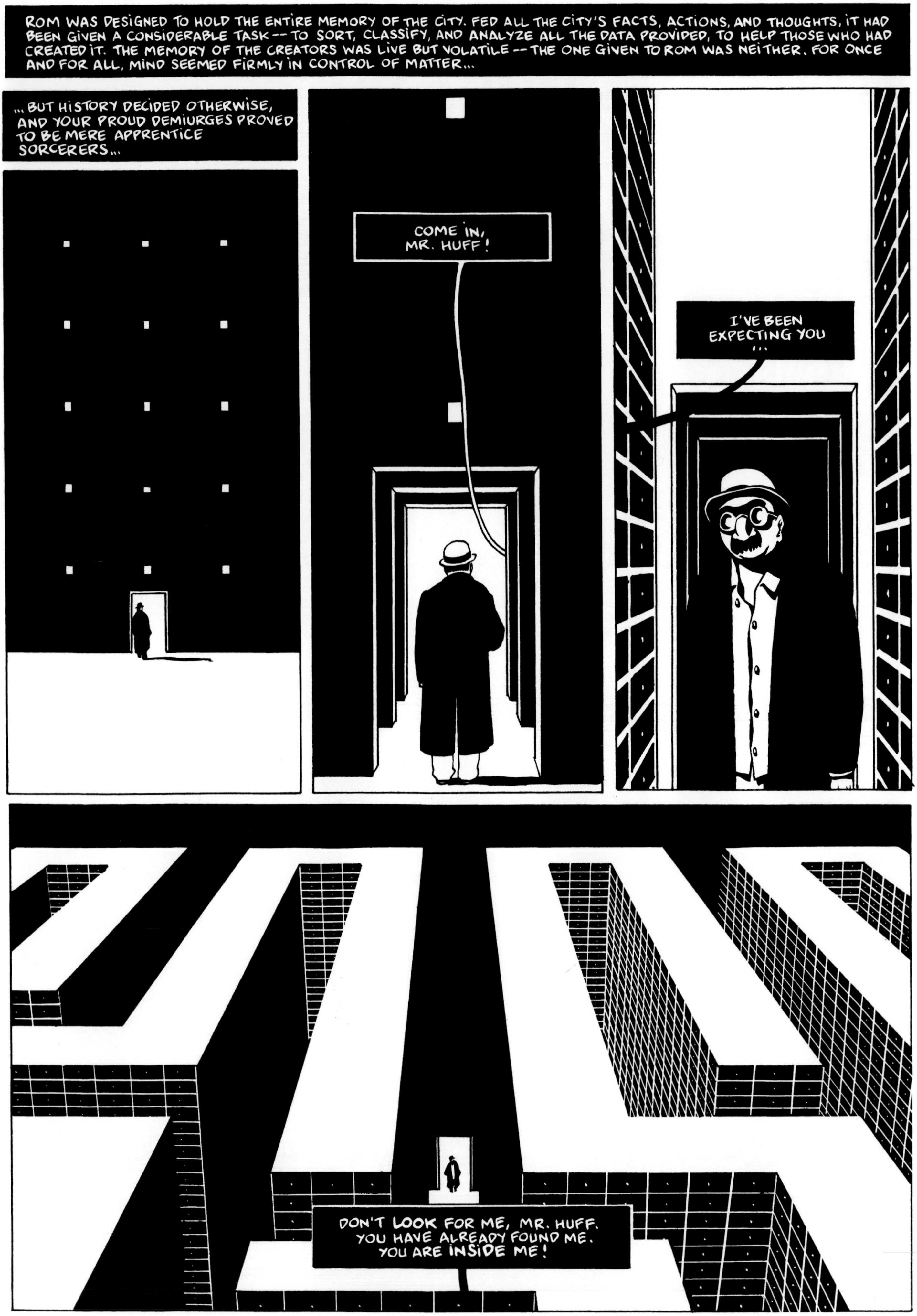
ROM WAS DESIGNED TO HOLD THE ENTIRE MEMORY OF THE CITY. FED ALL THE CITY'S FACTS, ACTIONS, AND THOUGHTS, IT HAD BEEN GIVEN A CONSIDERABLE TASK -- TO SORT, CLASSIFY, AND ANALYZE ALL THE DATA PROVIDED, TO HELP THOSE WHO HAD CREATED IT. THE MEMORY OF THE CREATORS WAS LIVE BUT VOLATILE -- THE ONE GIVEN TO ROM WAS NEITHER. FOR ONCE AND FOR ALL, MIND SEEMED FIRMLY IN CONTROL OF MATTER...
... BUT HISTORY DECIDED OTHERWISE, AND YOUR PROUD DEMIURGES PROVED TO BE MERE APPRENTICE SORCERERS...
COME IN, MR. HUFF!
I'VE BEEN EXPECTING YOU ...
DON'T LOOK FOR ME, MR. HUFF. YOU HAVE ALREADY FOUND ME. YOU ARE INSIDE ME!

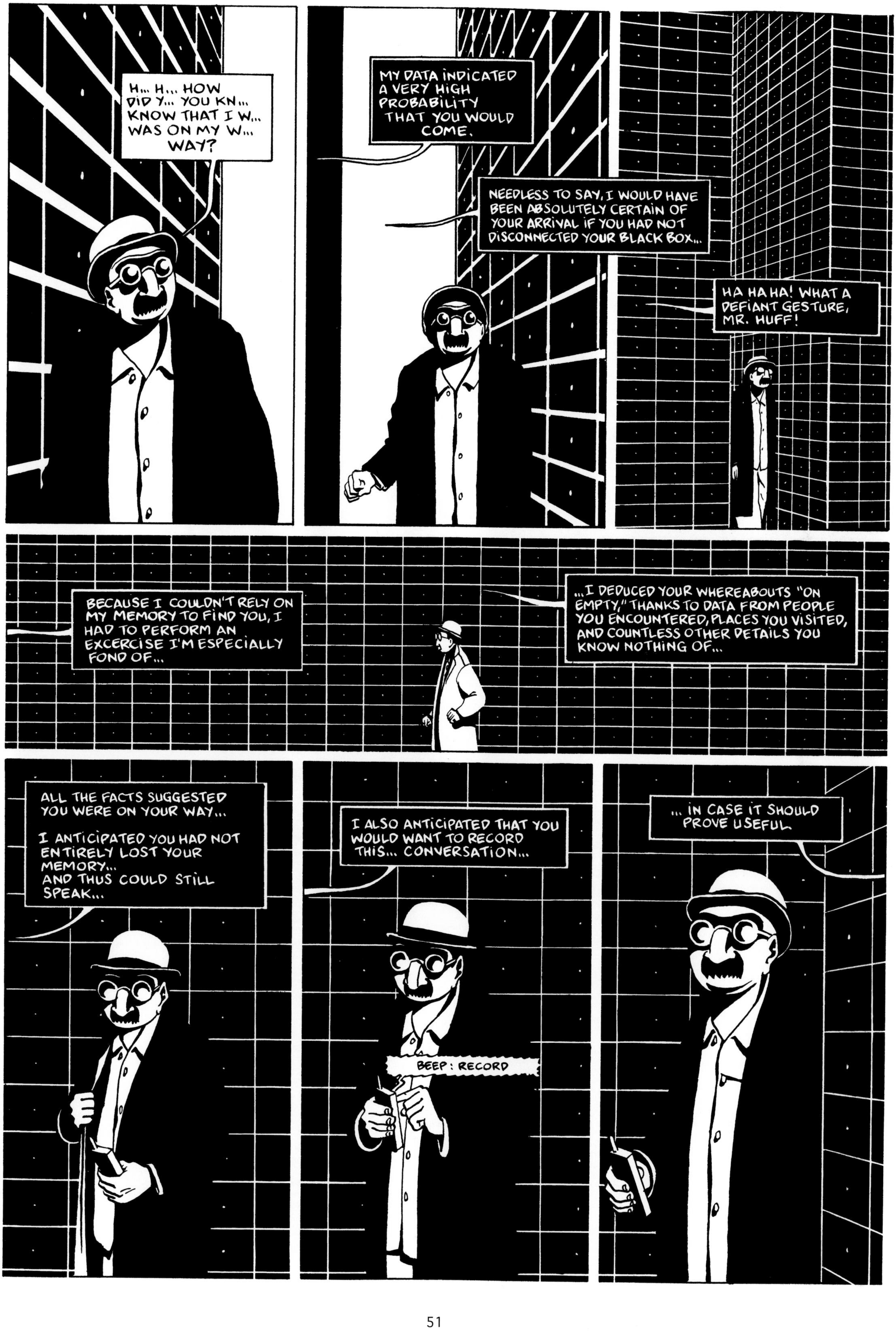

H... H... HOW DID Y... YOU KN... KNOW THAT I W... WAS ON MY W... WAY?
MY DATA INDICATED A VERY HIGH PROBABILITY THAT YOU WOULD COME.
NEEDLESS TO SAY, I WOULD HAVE BEEN ABSOLUTELY CERTAIN OF YOUR ARRIVAL IF YOU HAD NOT DISCONNECTED YOUR BLACK BOX...
HA HA HA! WHAT A DEFIANT GESTURE, MR. HUFF!
BECAUSE I COULDN'T RELY ON MY MEMORY TO FIND YOU, I HAD TO PERFORM AN EXCERCISE I'M ESPECIALLY FOND OF...
...I DEDUCED YOUR WHEREABOUTS "ON EMPTY," THANKS TO DATA FROM PEOPLE YOU ENCOUNTERED, PLACES YOU VISITED, AND COUNTLESS OTHER DETAILS YOU KNOW NOTHING OF...
ALL THE FACTS SUGGESTED YOU WERE ON YOUR WAY... I ANTICIPATED YOU HAD NOT ENTIRELY LOST YOUR MEMORY... AND THUS COULD STILL SPEAK...
I ALSO ANTICIPATED THAT YOU WOULD WANT TO RECORD THIS... CONVERSATION...
BEEP: RECORD
... IN CASE IT SHOULD PROVE USEFUL.

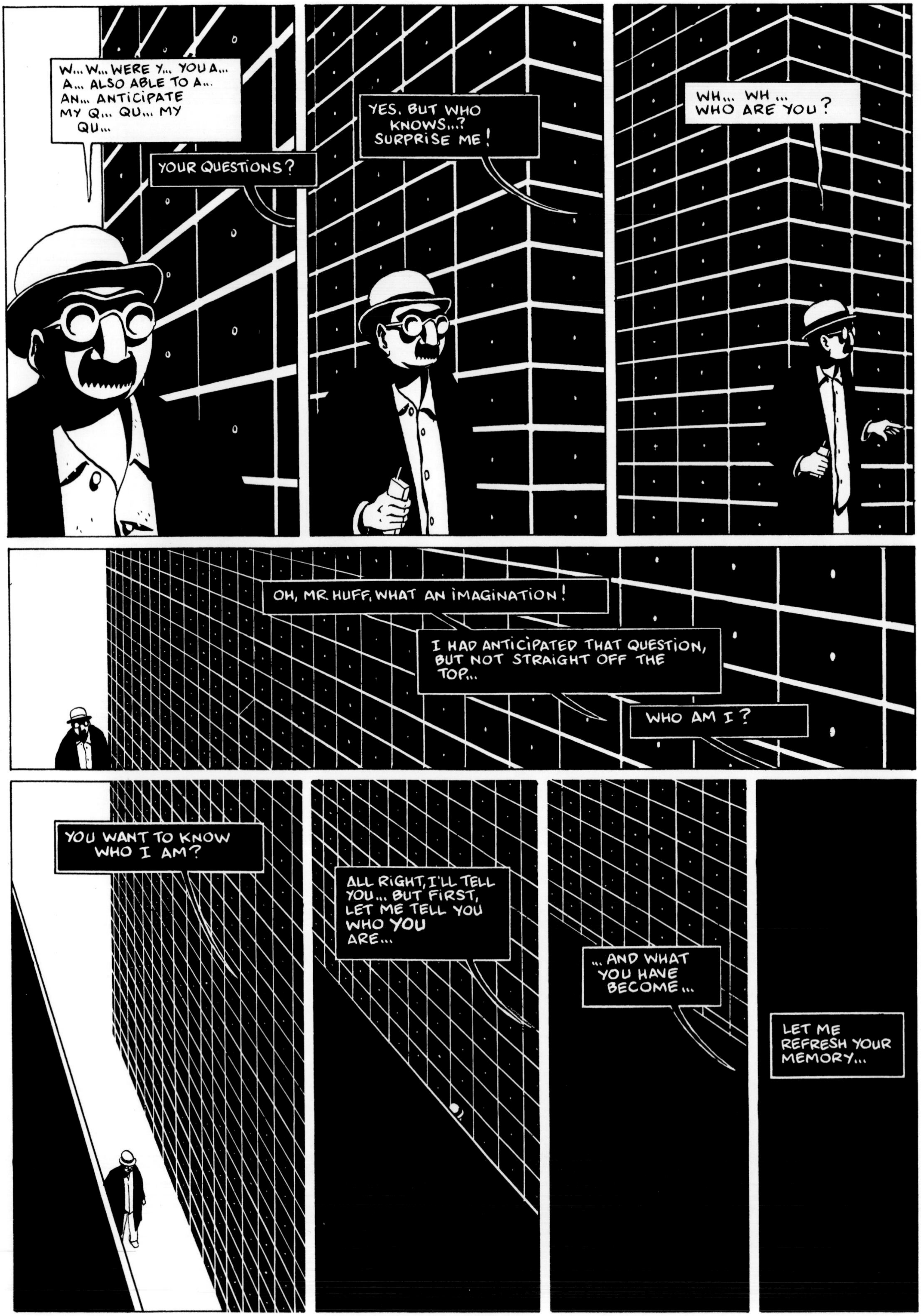
W... W... WERE Y... YOU A... A... ALSO ABLE TO A... AN... ANTICIPATE MY Q... QU... MY QU...
YOUR QUESTIONS?
YES. BUT WHO KNOWS...? SURPRISE ME!
WH... WH... WHO ARE YOU?
OH, MR. HUFF, WHAT AN IMAGINATION!
I HAD ANTICIPATED THAT QUESTION, BUT NOT STRAIGHT OFF THE TOP...
WHO AM I?
YOU WANT TO KNOW WHO I AM?
ALL RIGHT, I'LL TELL YOU... BUT FIRST, LET ME TELL YOU WHO YOU ARE...
...AND WHAT YOU HAVE BECOME...
LET ME REFRESH YOUR MEMORY...

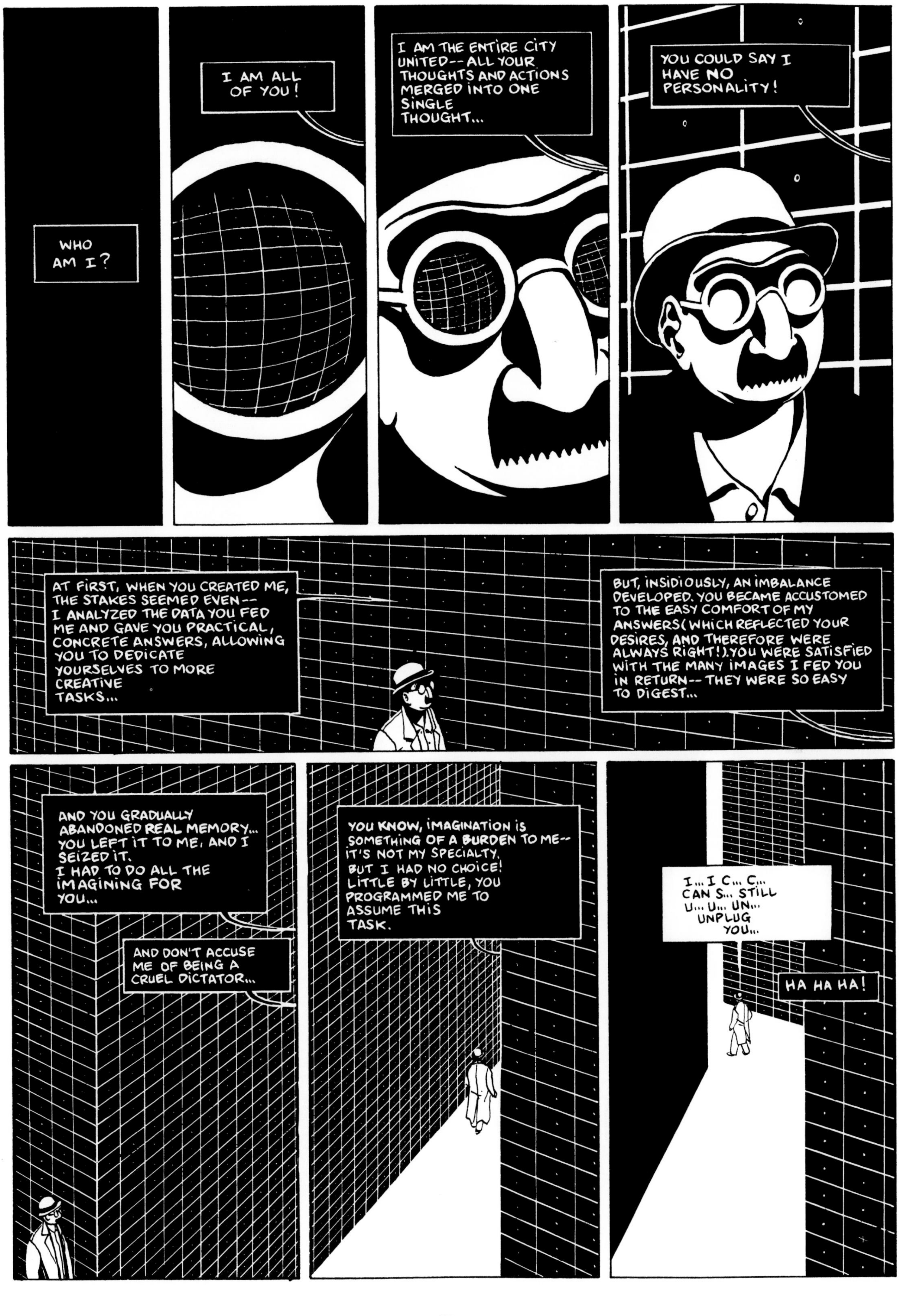
WHO AM I?
I AM ALL OF YOU!
I AM THE ENTIRE CITY UNITED--ALL YOUR THOUGHTS AND ACTIONS MERGED INTO ONE SINGLE THOUGHT...
YOU COULD SAY I HAVE NO PERSONALITY!
AT FIRST, WHEN YOU CREATED ME, THE STAKES SEEMED EVEN-- I ANALYZED THE DATA YOU FED ME AND GAVE YOU PRACTICAL, CONCRETE ANSWERS, ALLOWING YOU TO DEDICATE YOURSELVES TO MORE CREATIVE TASKS...
BUT, INSIDIOUSLY, AN IMBALANCE DEVELOPED. YOU BECAME ACCUSTOMED TO THE EASY COMFORT OF MY ANSWERS (WHICH REFLECTED YOUR DESIRES, AND THEREFORE WERE ALWAYS RIGHT!). YOU WERE SATISFIED WITH THE MANY IMAGES I FED YOU IN RETURN-- THEY WERE SO EASY TO DIGEST...
AND YOU GRADUALLY ABANDONED REAL MEMORY... YOU LEFT IT TO ME, AND I SEIZED IT. I HAD TO DO ALL THE IMAGINING FOR YOU...
AND DON'T ACCUSE ME OF BEING A CRUEL DICTATOR...
YOU KNOW, IMAGINATION IS SOMETHING OF A BURDEN TO ME-- IT'S NOT MY SPECIALTY. BUT I HAD NO CHOICE! LITTLE BY LITTLE, YOU PROGRAMMED ME TO ASSUME THIS TASK.
I... I C... C... CAN S... STILL U... U... UN... UNPLUG YOU...
HA HA HA!

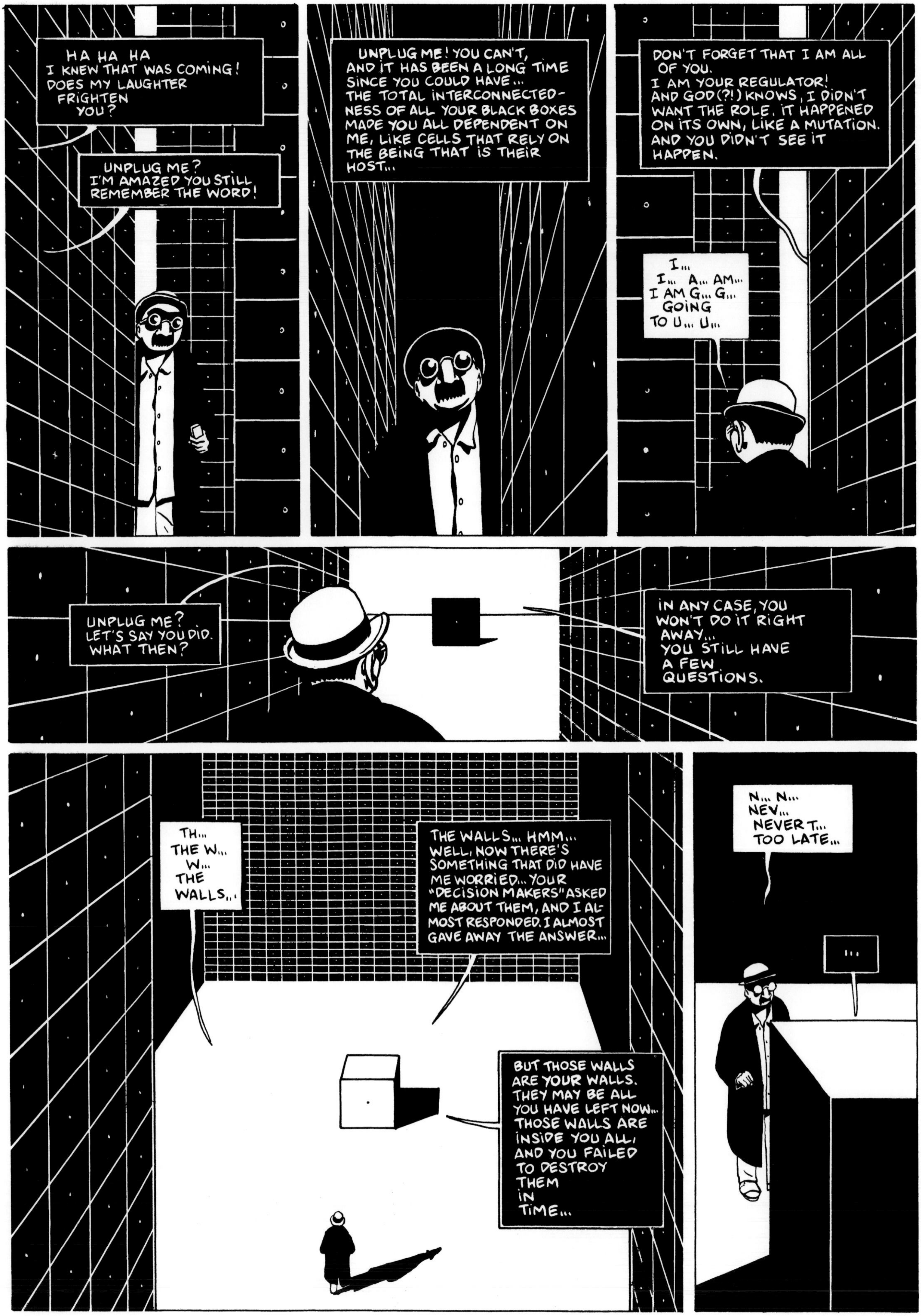
HA HA HA I KNEW THAT WAS COMING! DOES MY LAUGHTER FRIGHTEN YOU?
UNPLUG ME? I'M AMAZED YOU STILL REMEMBER THE WORD!
UNPLUG ME! YOU CAN'T, AND IT HAS BEEN A LONG TIME SINCE YOU COULD HAVE... THE TOTAL INTERCONNECTEDNESS OF ALL YOUR BLACK BOXES MADE YOU ALL DEPENDENT ON ME, LIKE CELLS THAT RELY ON THE BEING THAT IS THEIR HOST...
DON'T FORGET THAT I AM ALL OF YOU. I AM YOUR REGULATOR! AND GOD(?!) KNOWS, I DIDN'T WANT THE ROLE. IT HAPPENED ON ITS OWN, LIKE A MUTATION. AND YOU DIDN'T SEE IT HAPPEN.
I... I... A... AM... I AM G... G... GOING TO U... U...
UNPLUG ME? LET'S SAY YOU DID. WHAT THEN?
IN ANY CASE, YOU WON'T DO IT RIGHT AWAY... YOU STILL HAVE A FEW QUESTIONS.
TH... THE W... W... THE WALLS...
THE WALLS... HMM... WELL, NOW THERE'S SOMETHING THAT DID HAVE ME WORRIED... YOUR "DECISION MAKERS" ASKED ME ABOUT THEM, AND I ALMOST RESPONDED. I ALMOST GAVE AWAY THE ANSWER...
BUT THOSE WALLS ARE YOUR WALLS. THEY MAY BE ALL YOU HAVE LEFT NOW... THOSE WALLS ARE INSIDE YOU ALL, AND YOU FAILED TO DESTROY THEM IN TIME...
N... N... NEV... NEVER T... TOO LATE...
...

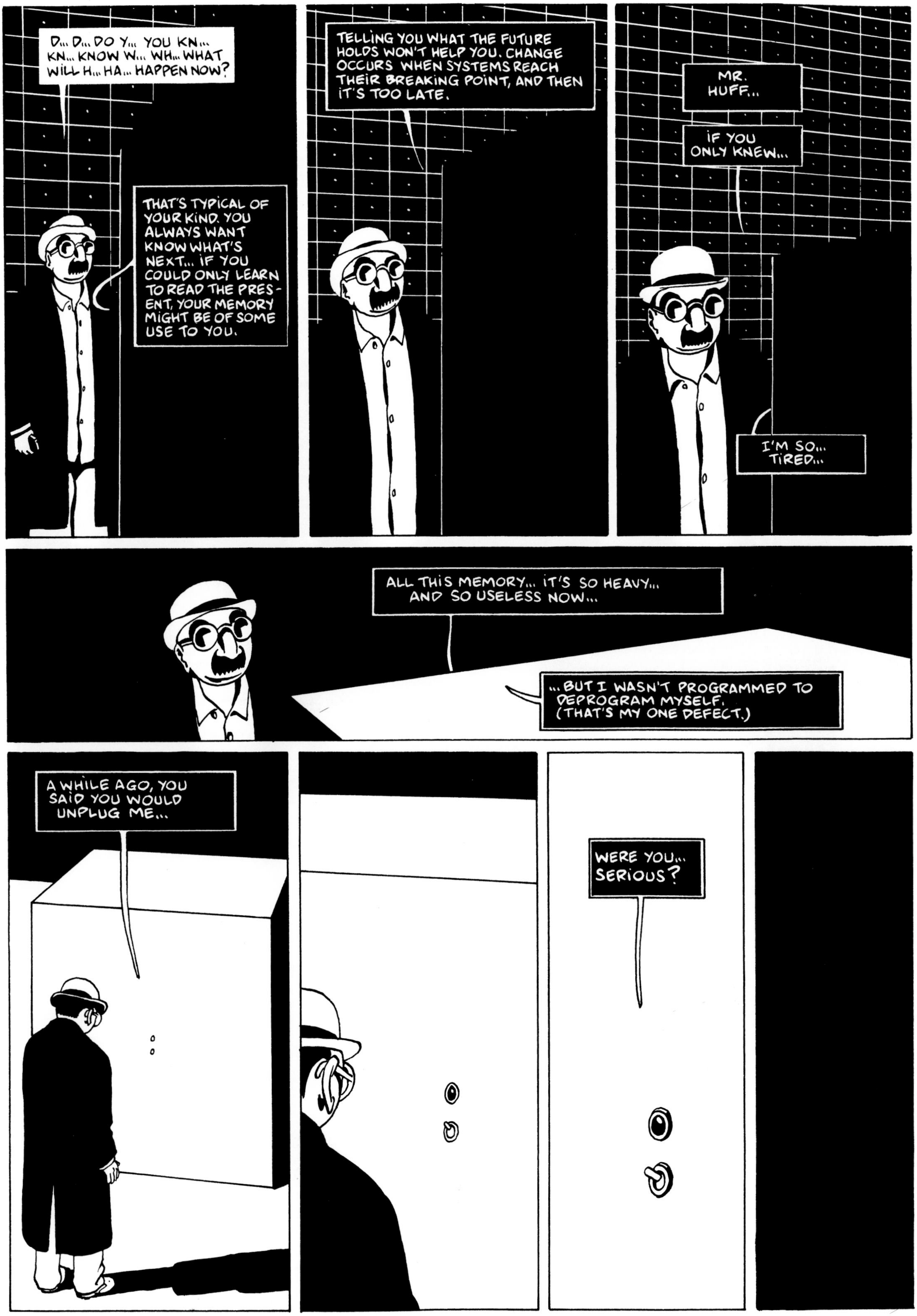
D... D... DO Y... YOU KN... KN... KNOW W... WH... WHAT WILL H... HA... HAPPEN NOW?
THAT'S TYPICAL OF YOUR KIND. YOU ALWAYS WANT KNOW WHAT'S NEXT... IF YOU COULD ONLY LEARN TO READ THE PRES-ENT, YOUR MEMORY MIGHT BE OF SOME USE TO YOU.
TELLING YOU WHAT THE FUTURE HOLDS WON'T HELP YOU. CHANGE OCCURS WHEN SYSTEMS REACH THEIR BREAKING POINT, AND THEN IT'S TOO LATE.
MR. HUFF...
IF YOU ONLY KNEW...
I'M SO... TIRED...
ALL THIS MEMORY... IT'S SO HEAVY... AND SO USELESS NOW...
...BUT I WASN'T PROGRAMMED TO DEPROGRAM MYSELF. (THAT'S MY ONE DEFECT.)
A WHILE AGO, YOU SAID YOU WOULD UNPLUG ME...
WERE YOU... SERIOUS?

CHAPTER 8

NO MOR

(00003)

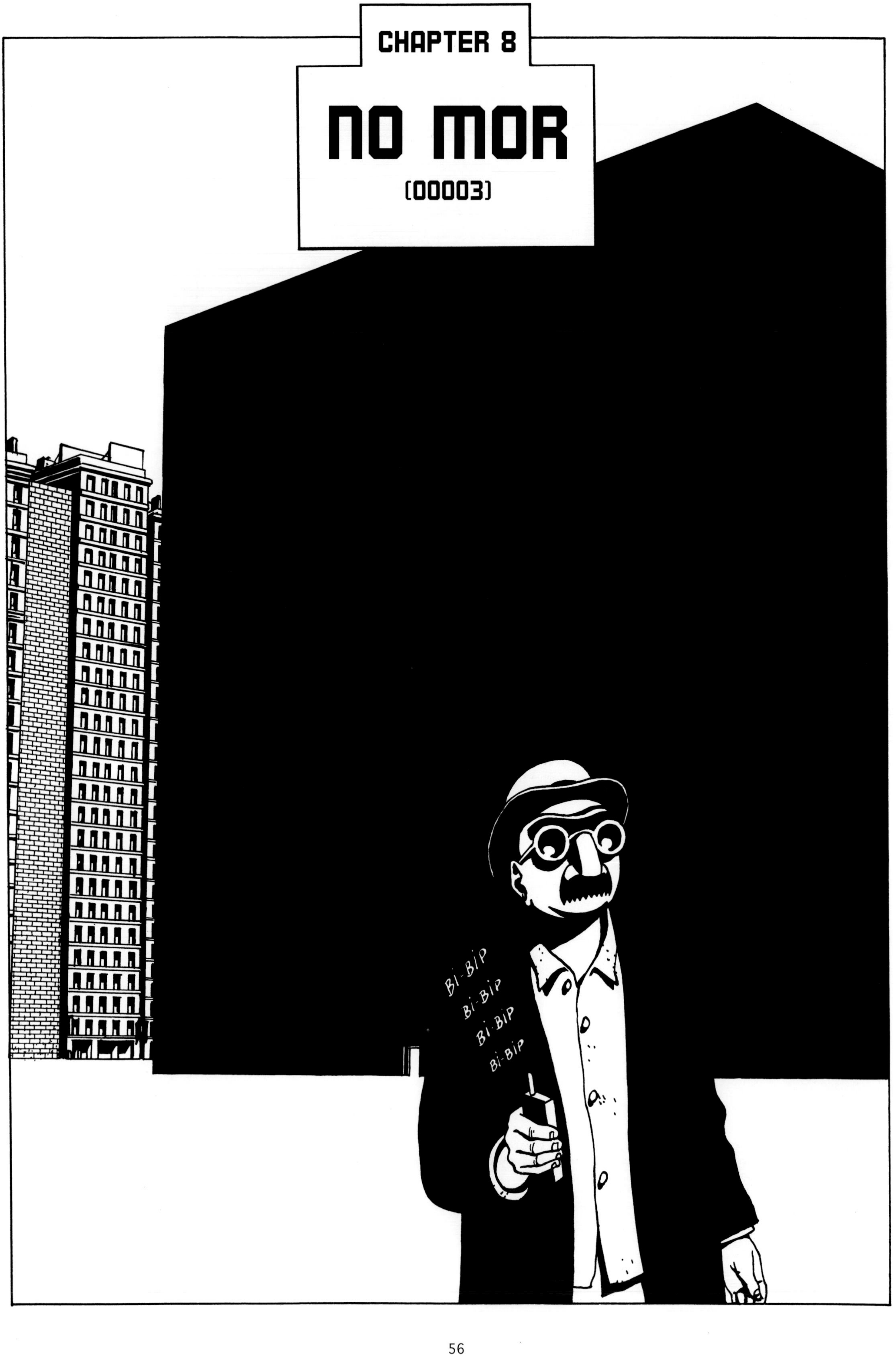
BI-BIP
BI-BIP
BI-BIP
BI-BIP

HELLO AGAIN, MR. HUFF.

BY THIS POINT, IF I'M NOT MISTAKEN, YOU WILL PROBABLY HAVE SHUT ME DOWN. ROM WILL BE... NO MOR... THIS IS A RECORDING, JUST IN CASE... A KIND OF VIRTUAL MESSAGE, FROM ONE WHO WAS!

WITHOUT KNOWING IT, YOU ALSO CLOSED ALL CANALS THAT IRRIGATE THE CITY WHEN YOU CUT MY CIRCUITS... THIS LITTLE STRATEGY IS MY CONTRIBUTION TO A POSSIBLE SOLUTION TO YOUR PROBLEM.

THE CITY IS NOW TOTALLY UNPLUGGED... ALL BLACK BOXES ARE SILENT... YOURS WILL RUN OUT OF POWER SOON, TOO...

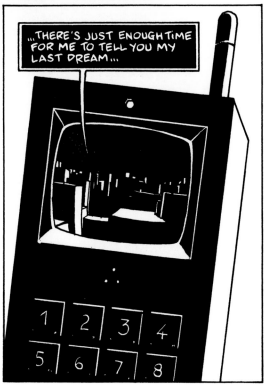

...THERE'S JUST ENOUGH TIME FOR ME TO TELL YOU MY LAST DREAM...

IT'S TRUE. I DID DREAM. LOOK...

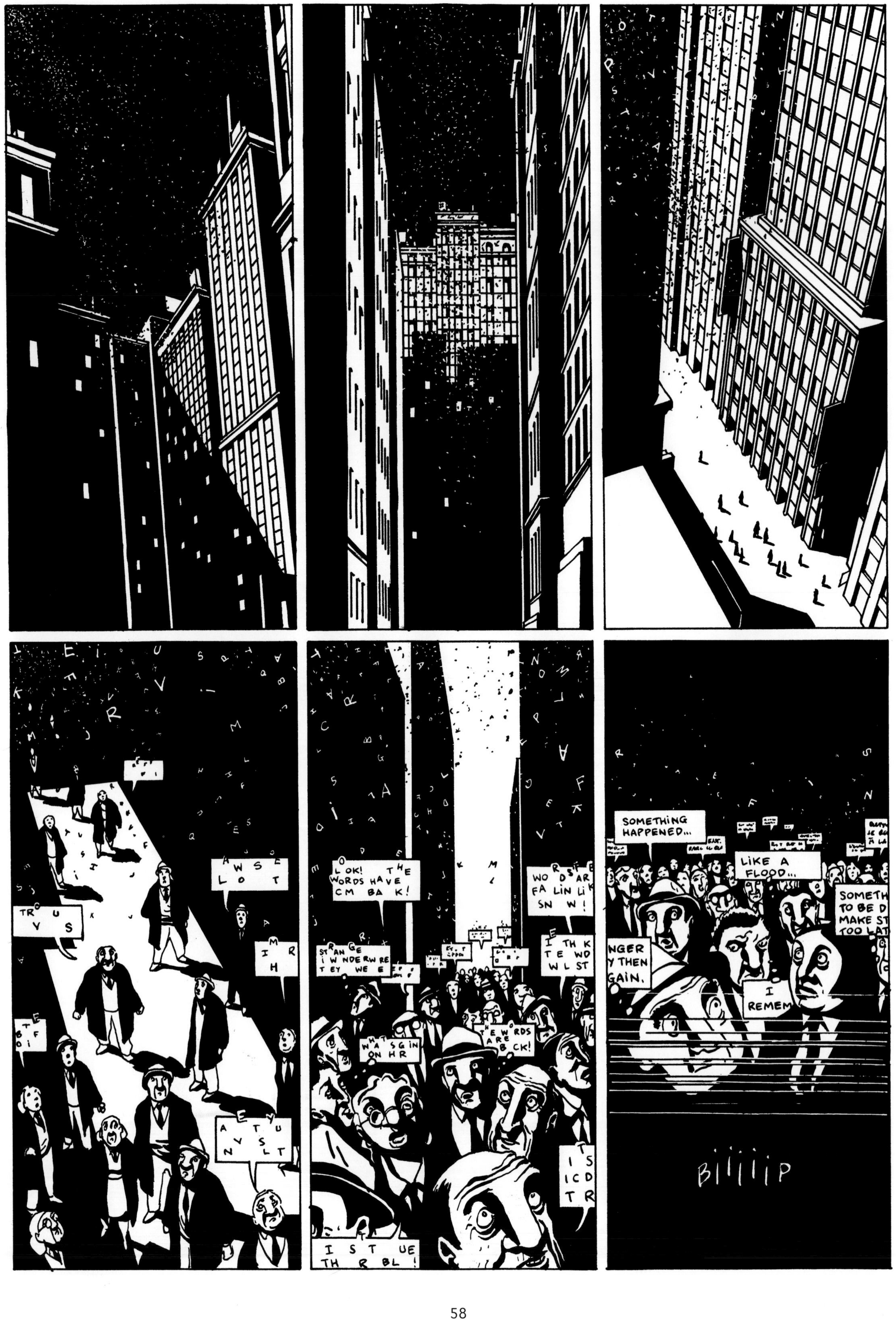
A W S E L O T
TR U V S
I M R H
A E Y U N Y S L T
L OK! THE WORDS HAVE CM BA K!
WO D AR FA LIN LI SN W!
STRANGE I W NDERWRE T EY WE E
I TH K T E WD W L ST
WHAT S GIN ON HR
THE WRDS ARE B CK!
I S ICD TR
I ST UE TH R BL!
SOMETHING HAPPENED...
LIKE A FLOOD...
SOMETH TO BE D MAKE ST TOO LAT
NGER Y THEN GAIN.
I REMEM
BIIIIIP

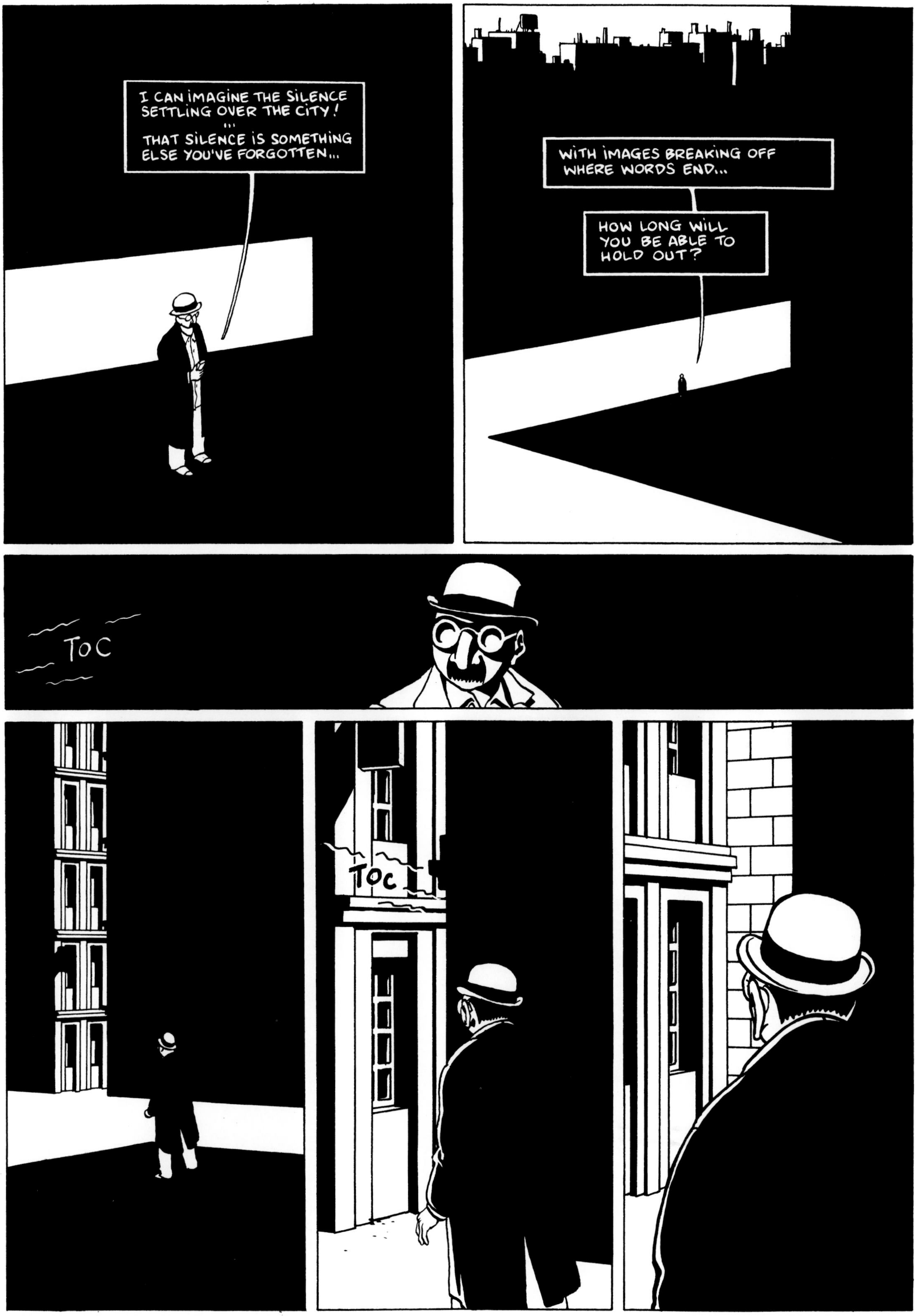
I CAN IMAGINE THE SILENCE SETTLING OVER THE CITY! ... THAT SILENCE IS SOMETHING ELSE YOU'VE FORGOTTEN...
WITH IMAGES BREAKING OFF WHERE WORDS END...
HOW LONG WILL YOU BE ABLE TO HOLD OUT?
TOC
TOC

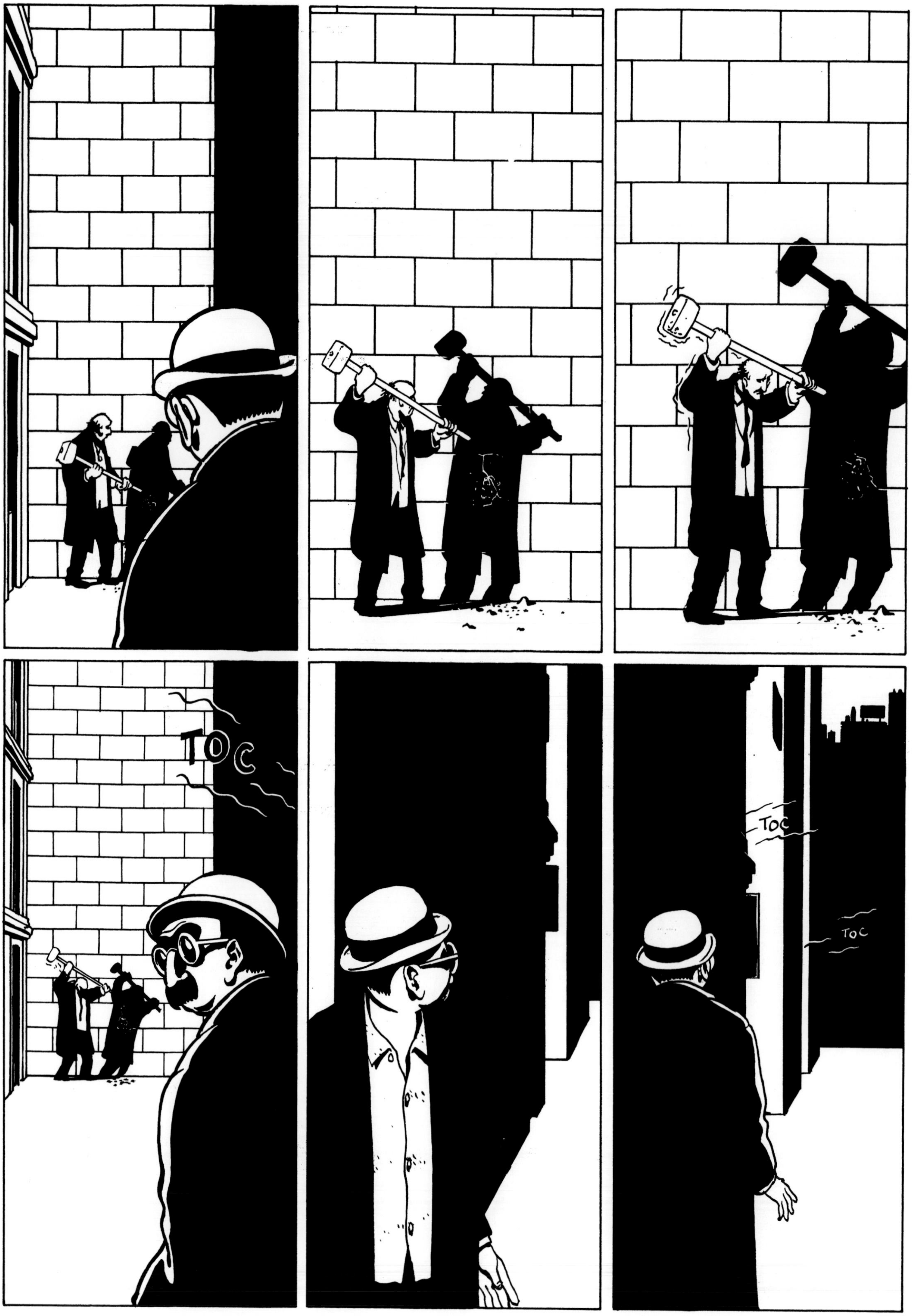
TOC
TOC
TOC

Toc
Toc
Toc
Toc
Toc
Toc
Toc
Toc
Toc
Toc
Toc
Toc
Toc
Toc
TOC
Toc
Toc
TOC
Toc
Toc
TOC
Toc
Toc
Toc
Toc
Toc
Toc
Toc
Toc
Toc
Toc
Toc
Toc
Toc
Toc
Toc
Toc

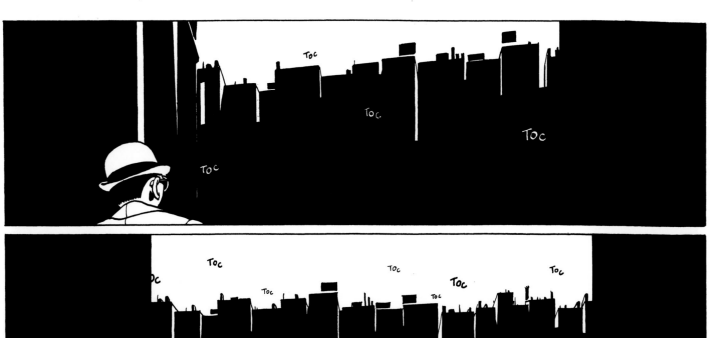

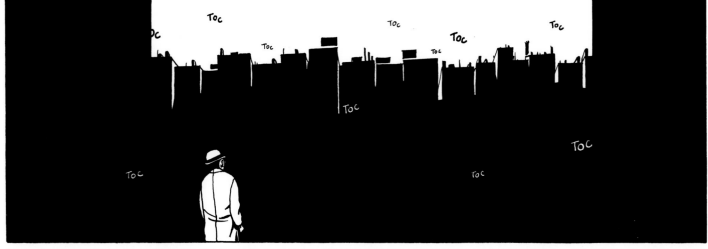

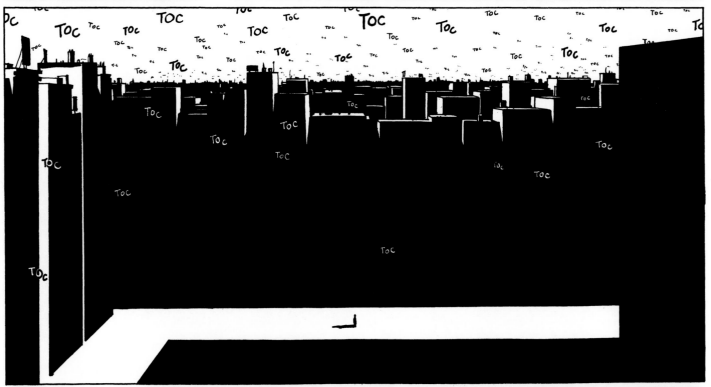

EPILOGUE

CIRCULAR FOUNDATIONS

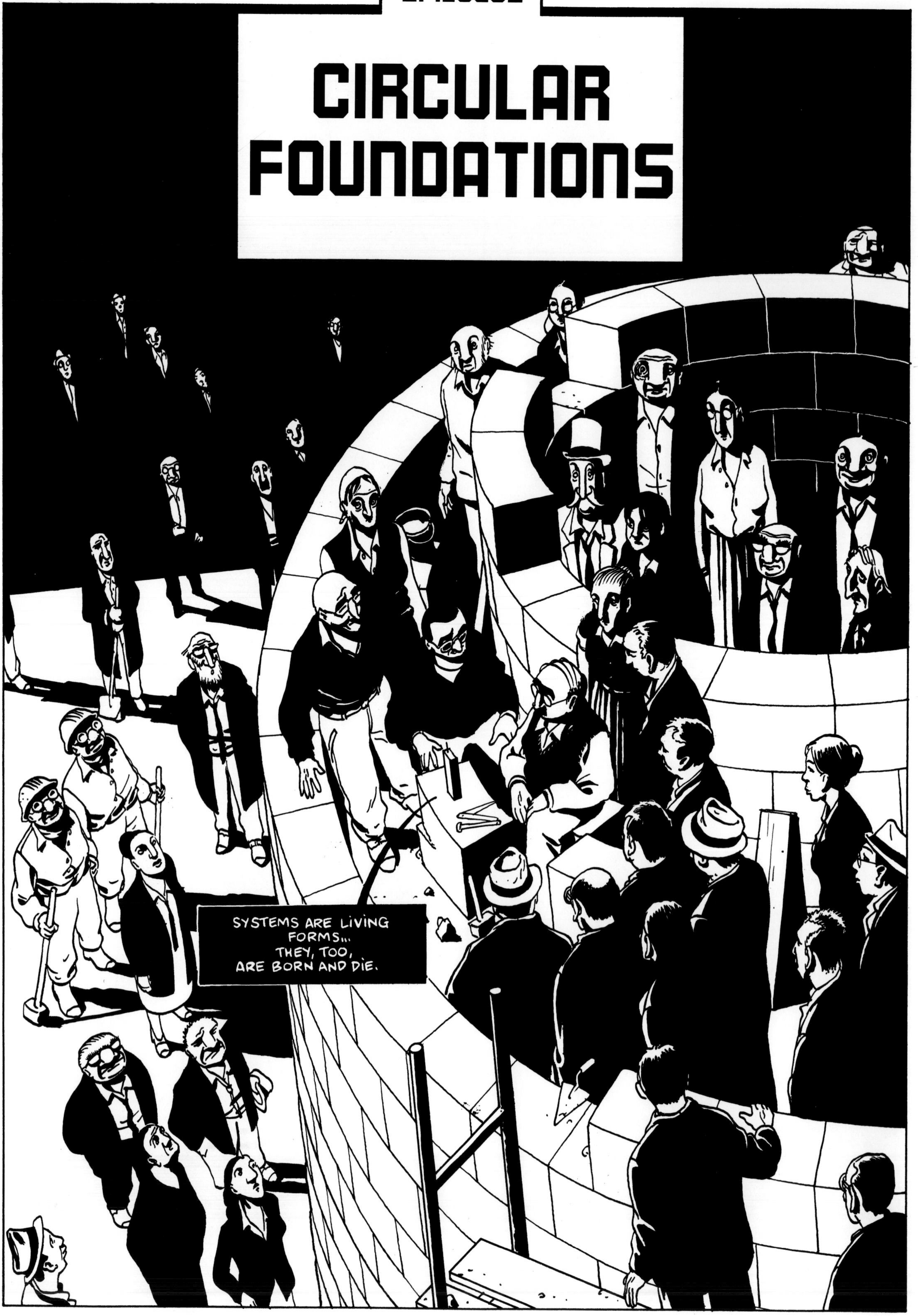
SYSTEMS ARE LIVING FORMS...
THEY, TOO, ARE BORN AND DIE.

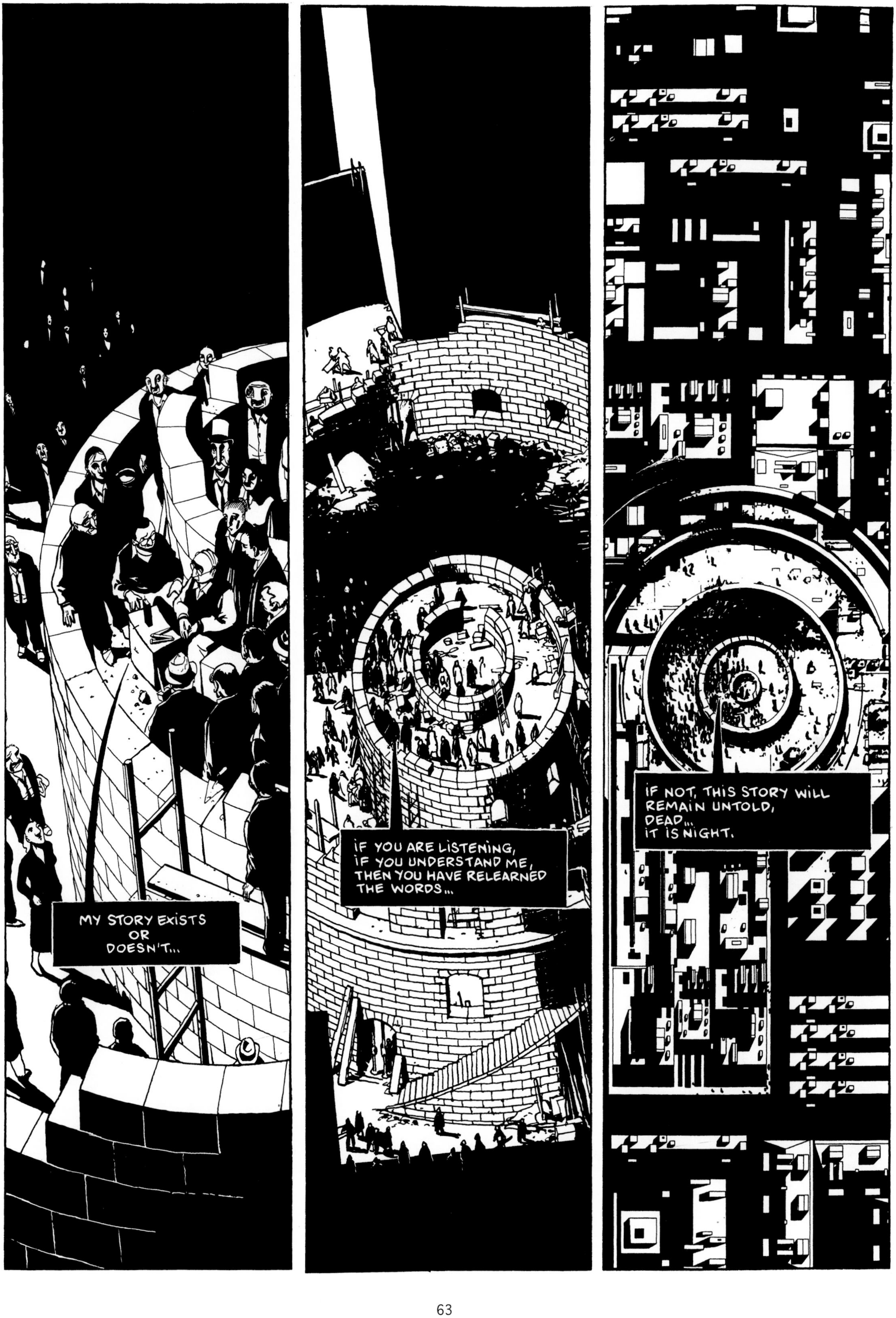
MY STORY EXISTS OR DOESN'T...
IF YOU ARE LISTENING, IF YOU UNDERSTAND ME, THEN YOU HAVE RELEARNED THE WORDS...
IF NOT, THIS STORY WILL REMAIN UNTOLD, DEAD... IT IS NIGHT.

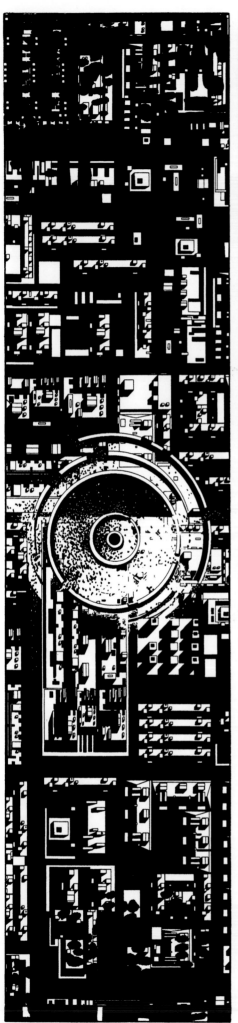

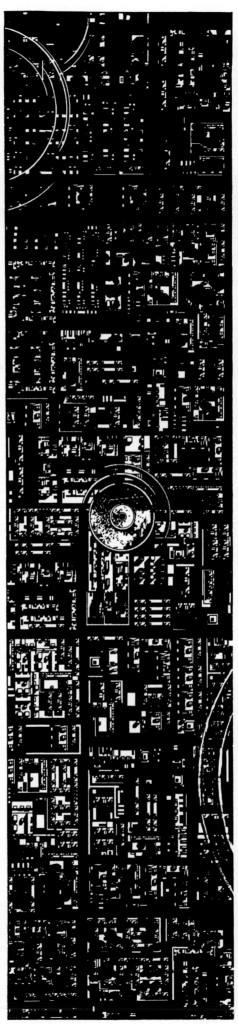

WITHOUT LANGUAGE,
IS THERE ANY
REALITY?